D0325117

"An outstandi.., ... important and timely topic..."

Sooner or later we all face the probability of caring for a loved one older than ourselves, although we like to pretend it will never happen to us. Joyce has given us, through her own personal experiences and those of others, rich insights in the care of the aging with helpful steps to encourage and guide us in making that caregiving time a positive experience for the caregiver as well as the care-receiver. I have worked with Joyce and observed her true heart for people. Her words of wisdom will be helpful. *WHEN PARENTS GROW OLD* is an outstanding book on an important and timely topic.

> Florence Littauer
> President, CLASS Speakers, Inc.

This is more than just another how-to-do-it book. The author has interpreted the reality of caregiving in a warm, personal and honest way. There is an excellent balance between helpful information and real feelings. It will help the caregiver understand and cope with feelings as well as find needed resources and make important decisions. It is like having a friend at your side to share with you and "walk" you through the caregiving experience.

> E. E. "Red" Evans
> Administrative Assistant
> Narramore Christian Foundation

Of all the life tasks we must face, I know of no other that brings to the surface the multiplicity of powerful emotions as does caring for aged loved ones. Joyce Althens Minatra allows the reader to experience the lessons learned through an intimate look at her own relationships that is both practical and reassuring. She effectively communi-

cates the truth learned by so many that suffering pro-
duces spiritual growth and while the life task of caring for
the aged is a demanding one, it can be faced with faith,
hope and love.

> Steven L. Dowdle, Ed.D.
> Counseling Psychologist
> Co-host, "Today's Family" radio program

WHEN PARENTS GROW OLD is a book that every caregiver
needs. It is most practical in its approach, and proves
more than helpful on every page. It shows the caregiver
not only how to care for the aging loved ones, but also
begins with an excellent section on the "feelings" of the
caregiver as well as the aging loved one. As a pastor I will
recommend this book to my congregation and friends—
and all caregivers as *the* book to aid them in fulfilling this
vital ministry.

> Franklin Bixler, Pastor
> Westside Christian Church
> Long Beach, California

Joyce's tender heart and concern for others compel her
to write to every child whose parents are growing up too
soon. The dramatic shift from being the child of my parents to taking care of my parents is powerfully told in a
manner that is certain to encourage and enlighten every
reader. I recommend this book wholeheartedly to every
person whose parents are growing older before their eyes.

> Roger Barrier, Pastor
> Casas Adobes Baptist Church
> Tucson, Arizona

WHEN PARENTS GROW OLD

Joyce Althens Minatra

Here's Life Publishers

First Printing, August 1992

Published by
HERE'S LIFE PUBLISHERS, INC.
P. O. Box 1576
San Bernardino, CA 92402

© 1992, Joyce Althens Minatra
All rights reserved
Printed in the United States of America

Cover design by David Marty Design
Typesetting by Genesis Publications

Library of Congress Cataloging-in-Publication Data
Minatra, Joyce Althens.
   When parents grow old / Joyce Althens Minatra.
      p.   cm.
   ISBN 0-89840-305-7
   1. Aging parents—Home care—United States. 2. Parent and adult
child—United States. 3. Caregivers—United States. 4. Aging parents—
Family relationships—United States. I. Title.
HV1461.M56 1992
362.6—dc20   92-13566
                            CIP

Upon the release of each new book, Here's Life Publishers sponsors the planting of a tree through Global ReLeaf™ a program of the American Forestry Association.

Scripture quotations designated NASB are from *The New American Standard Bible,* © The Lockman Foundation 1960, 1962, 1963, 1968, 1971, 1972, 1975, 1977.
Scripture quotations designated KJV are from the *King James Version.*
Scripture quotations designated TLB are from *The Living Bible.* © 1971 by Tyndale House Publishers, Wheaton, Illinois.

For More Information, Write:
L.I.F.E.—P.O. Box A399, Sydney South 2000, Australia
Campus Crusade for Christ of Canada—Box 300, Vancouver, B.C., V6C 2X3, Canada
Campus Crusade for Christ—Pearl Assurance House, 4 Temple Row, Birmingham, B2 5HG, England
Lay Institute for Evangelism—P.O. Box 8786, Auckland 3, New Zealand
Campus Crusade for Christ—P.O. Box 240, Raffles City Post Office, Singapore 9117
Great Commission Movement of Nigeria—P.O. Box 500, Jos, Plateau State Nigeria, West Africa
Campus Crusade for Christ International—100 Sunport Lane, Orlando, FL 32809, U.S.A.

Dedicated to my beloved
Mom and Pop
who were the inspiration for this book,
and from whom I learned some lessons of love.

Contents

—

Acknowledgments

A book is never accomplished by the author alone. There are those who help, encourage, and pray, and without them writing would be a lonely task.

I gratefully acknowledge my children, Lee and Suzie Althens and Brian and Lori Lee, who have encouraged me with love and prayers, always believing I could do it. Their pride in me has kept me writing.

I am thankful for my family of brothers and sisters who have supported me in my efforts, and gladly shared their personal experiences with me.

I especially appreciate the day-to-day love and encouragement of my husband, Jack.

To my friends who shared their personal stories, who loved me, encouraged me, and prayed for me, I am grateful.

I am grateful for the gracious help of Marilyn Heavilin in the very beginning of this book. Her professional critique and appropriate suggestions were motivators when discouragement hit, and her words, "Congratulations! I think you have a book," were music to keep playing to.

It all began with the greatest motivator I've known, Florence Littauer. She has inspired me with godly wisdom both personally and through her Christian Leaders and Speakers seminars.

It was the Lord Jesus Christ, however, who empowered me to birth this book by combining my experiences with the talent and ability He gave me.

1

A Critical Time of Life

My mother loved the ocean. She had been brought up as a young girl by the sea, but when her family moved to New Hampshire and she married my father, she never knew those days again. Sometimes she told us of the good times she and her sisters and friends experienced in Rhode Island, and I think she longed for a glimpse of the ocean.

During the years of caring for my parents, we often took rides, heading for the Atlantic. While we ambled slowly along the coast, Mom would roll down her window, breathe deeply of the fresh salt air, and exclaim how good it smelled. She experienced those times with all her senses, and it brought her joy. We would find a place to eat overlooking the rocks and churning surf and enjoy lunch together.

My father was not a lover of the sea in the same way my mother was, but he was content to ride and look without the responsibility of driving. He commented on the old stone walls, wondering who had built them. In his halting way, he would remark on the growth of the trees and how fields with stone walls had given way to woods.

He enjoyed riding past old familiar places that held memories and talking of people, some long gone, and incidents in his life. We reminisced about the times he took me with him when he read meters for the power company, once stopping at a place where the pigs and chickens had free run of the house.

When I think about my parents, I often remember times like that and smile. And though our final years together were occasionally difficult and frustrating, we had our good times as well. I loved my parents and grieved deeply the summer of 1976 when they died within a week of each other.

When the Unexpected Happens to You

I was in my forties when my caregiving responsibilities began, and I was not ready. I was not ready to have my dynamic, independent, hardworking parents become old. Suddenly, or so it seemed, they were no longer vital. They were slowed by age and infirmity. They had become dependent on others for the basic needs of life.

These dear people had been the backdrop of my life, always there for me, offering security just by being my parents, supporting and encouraging my efforts, tolerating and overlooking my brash, know-it-all ways, and loving me. Now they were weak and infirm. I had never thought of old age happening to *my* parents.

Do you feel this way? Are you struggling under the burden of caring for an aging loved one? I know I could hardly face the grief as I watched my beautiful mother and vital father become increasingly dependent. I was constantly blaming myself, thinking that somehow I could have kept this from happening. All the things I felt I could have and should have done goaded me.

Age is not an attractive prospect. During those caregiving years, I myself reached mid-life—that bridge between youth and old age—and it was shocking for me. I looked at my mom and dad and saw my future. I looked at my son and daughter and saw my past. My parents were growing old and needing me more. My children were growing up and needing me less. My life was in turmoil, and there were a few times when I wasn't sure I was going to make it.

The Events That Changed My Life

In my late thirties, I took advantage of some free time by returning to college to complete my degree. I began with two courses to see if I was still mentally functional after twenty years. My father, at sixty-eight, enrolled in the writing course with me. We enjoyed the challenge and the competitiveness.

I admired my dad for his desire to continue learning. He had taken advantage of his early retirement to serve the community as a Selectman and in the State Legislature. We talked about his returning to college full-time with me to earn our degrees together. However, on a wintry January evening, on our way to class, my father suffered a slight stroke. His eyes were bloodshot and his face fiery. Earlier at my house he'd been unable to speak for a few minutes, but he insisted on going because it was exam night. He talked incessantly during the twenty-five-mile trip to class and on the way home.

When we arrived home, he said, "I think I've had a little stroke." Before I could protest, he was in his car and drove down the icy hill to the farm twenty miles away.

Shaking with fear and agonizing over my stupidity, I raced frantically up the steep, snow-covered driveway and called my mother. Finally he arrived home safely, but the next day he had a second stroke that paralyzed his right side and affected his speech and communication. Our lives were changed forever.

For the next few weeks I studied at the farm while watching over my dad. My life became divided into sections: wife, mother, caregiver and student. When the grades were given out, Pop received a *C* for the course because he had passed his last exam.

He continued to improve and we were encouraged to see him try hard to regain his strength. I enrolled in a full schedule of courses, determined to finish—as much for him as for myself. Then a month later he suffered another stroke that was even more debilitating. We tried to rehabilitate him but he lost his motivation. He was able to walk and care for himself but never regained his ability to write or communicate effectively.

I prayed that he would live to see me graduate, and I promised a God I didn't know that I would care for my mother and father the rest of their lives.

A New Decade

My decision to return to college came at a time when my marriage of almost twenty years was threadbare and my self-esteem was extremely low. I also had to face my children leaving home.

The June after my father's stroke, my son Lee graduated from high school, and the next day he left New Hampshire to drive to Alaska with a friend. I admired his adventuresome spirit, but my heart ached as I watched him drive away, and I cried. I looked forward to his return in the fall.

However, when fall came, my eighteen-year-old son—a shaggy-haired kid in blue jeans—joined the Coast Guard. It was a difficult separation that took time to adjust to. I went to school with fear and trembling, feeling that I might fail, and I studied hard to fill the emptiness in my life.

During the days of commuting the fifty miles, I began to think about God and the purpose of my life. One time I felt hopeless almost to the point of suicide.

I began visiting churches feeling that the answer lay there. On a sunny April day in 1970, in a little country church, I found the love and forgiveness I'd been searching for in the Person of Jesus Christ. But my life didn't change much. Although I went to church and read the Bible, I lacked the courage to right the wrongs in my personal life and in my marriage.

One week before graduation, on the way home from a celebration dinner, my husband fell asleep at the wheel and we had an accident. It totaled our car, but miraculously we had few injuries. I was sure God was speaking to me through this incident, yet my life continued as before.

Two and a half years after enrolling in college, just after my fortieth birthday, I graduated *cum laude* with a B.A. degree. Pop was there with tears streaming down his face. He gripped my hand with his strong left hand as I filed past his seat to receive my diploma.

Two weeks later my daughter was involved in another serious accident, but neither she nor her friend were injured. That day I felt compelled to commit my life to Jesus Christ. Almost instantly my life took a new direction. New desires replaced the old self-centered ones. I wanted to be God's woman, to be the wife He wanted me to be, and to live according to His purpose.

Soon after this the Lord brought my sixteen-year-old niece to live with us, and then later, a sixteen-year-old boy. Both needed a home. I began to learn about the love of God.

A new decade had begun, and in me a new life began, too. It was a decade of beginnings and endings, sorrows and joys. Without the strength of the Lord, the next years would have been almost impossible.

While I was attempting to cope with the grief of both my father's stroke and Lee's leaving home, dealing with guilt for my failures, working on rebuilding my marriage relationship, and trying to meet the needs of my teenage daughter as well as two others, I was faced with what I envisioned as the straw that would break the camel's back. My ninety-two-year-old grandmother, "Nanny," could no longer live alone and moved in with my folks on the farm.

I prayed for an answer to the problems that were created with that move—my sparrow-like mother caring for a disabled husband and a demanding mother-in-law. I became the answer to my own prayers.

We moved Nanny to a care facility near our home. She wasn't happy there, but she wouldn't have been happy anywhere. She had lived in the same house for most of her life, and now that life had been disrupted. She was separated from everything and everyone familiar, and from her hometown where her friends called her "Winnie."

I visited her regularly, took her shopping and to church, and each time she asked if I would take her home in the spring. I knew she couldn't go home in the spring or any time, but how could I tell her? I realized how awful and how final it must be never to go home again. And once again I agonized with guilt because I felt responsible for Nanny's situation. I didn't want the additional burden of her care but it was thrust upon me and I felt trapped, hedged in on all sides by the obligations.

Becoming a Part of "The Sandwich Generation"

There was no help available to me as I struggled through those difficult years. I felt so alone. Fortunately, that's not the case now for others facing this situation. There are research studies, articles and books that support and encourage those in this stage of life.

Edwin Kiester, Jr. calls this generation of caregivers "The Sandwich Generation." He says,

> The "sandwich generation" is the colorful title given to those squeezed between conflicting and competing needs of the generation above and the generation below. According to one accepted estimate, five million Americans constitute the "meat" in the "sandwich," going without vacations, shortcutting their own careers, often mortgaging hard-earned savings for their own retirement while struggling to assist their ailing, aging parents.[1]

It was not until after the deaths of my grandmother and my parents that I began to think about the feelings I had agonized over. And I realized also that I wasn't alone. I know now that there are many others facing heart-rending caregiving responsibilities. There are millions struggling with similar feelings. You are probably one of them.

How much better to acknowledge and understand those feelings and deal with them as you go. The way those feelings are handled along the way affects the attitudes and behavior of the aged ones and the caregiver toward one another, toward themselves, and toward life.

After extensive research and study on this subject, I realize now that the last stage of my loved ones' lives could have been a more joyful time for them and for me—if only I had known then what I know now. It is my prayer that what I have learned will help you where you are right now.

—

Take a sheet of paper and write down your feelings about being a caregiver. Be honest. List your frustrations and your complaints. List also the joys and the blessings.

2

Dealing With Decisions

A s my children left home and my parents grew older, I found myself struggling with a mixture of feelings I didn't understand or even recognize until years later. I realize now that I was moving from nurturer to supporter. My role became blurred as I, the child, became the authority in the lives of those who had always represented authority in my life. It was awkward for me as well as for my parents, and it caused stress and anxiety.

This reversed authority role also added a weight of guilt. It was almost as if I had taken something from my parents that didn't belong to me.

I felt frustrated and helpless as I tried to keep Mom and Dad independent, attempting to make decisions that would be the most acceptable and the least humiliating. I wanted them to continue living by themselves, making their own decisions. After all, they were infirm only in their bodies, not in their minds. How much should I expect from them, and how much should I do?

I'm sure you've experienced the fear of making wrong choices, of not doing what's best for your loved ones. When they are looking to you for the next step, and when they are helpless without you, it becomes a heavy responsibility.

I'd like to share with you some of the decision-making processes my family and others like us went through. We didn't always make the perfect choices, and we'd probably

19

do some things differently if we had to do them over again. But what we learned may help you—and save you from some of the heartbreak we experienced.

Tailor Your Solution to Your Situation

My father's dependent condition meant there were some basic needs that had to be met immediately. Suddenly he could no longer drive, so Mom, who had suffered a heart condition and painful arthritis and also couldn't drive, had to depend on others. Pop wasn't able to mow the lawns or tend the gardens; Mom could no longer manage the stairs to the cellar to do the laundry. Vacuuming and cleaning were also out of the question for her limited strength. Although Mom and Dad were capable of getting their meals and tending daily needs, I did the laundry, shopping, cleaning and yard work. Eventually I cooked meals that could be warmed in the oven.

Despite our precautions, Mom fell several times, fracturing her knees, elbow and hip. As she grew more fragile, I tended to become overprotective. Unfortunately, while trying to keep them independent, I didn't make allowances for their emotional needs. One day my mother went upstairs just to look through familiar and remembered things in their loft. She went up cautiously, sitting from one step to the next. When she told me about her adventure, I humiliated her with my anger about taking such chances. I realize now that I should have praised her courage and cautioned her gently, offering to go with her the next time.

Other decisions once made by my folks fell to me. Mom had taken care of the finances for many years and it was a prideful point with her. She enjoyed her "accounts." However, when Mom was stricken with congestive heart failure, we opened a joint account, giving me the authority to take care of their obligations and personal needs. I felt as if I had stripped them of more independence and privacy, but it was the only solution we found workable in our situation.

We also made a decision to hire a live-in woman to cook for them and do some of the housework. My father was against the idea. The woman was bossy, and she tried to regiment when they got up in the morning, ate their meals, and went to bed. They were no longer free or comfortable in their own home. We realized that it was better for them to live by themselves and move at their own pace without the stress of trying to meet someone else's expectations.

Has your family tried various solutions to your situations? Don't be afraid to admit when a poor decision has been made. Although having a woman live in would have relieved my stress and workload, it wasn't the best solution for my folks. Each family situation must be handled based on its members' individual personalities and needs.

My friend Jim lived with and cared for his grandmother for ten years until she reached her nineties and became more and more infirm. Jim tried to work his real estate job and take care of all of his Granny's personal needs. He cooked her meals in the morning and evening; others brought meals at noon. When Granny became incontinent, he changed her diapers and cleaned up messes in her bed and in the bathroom.

After a talk with his father, Jim hired a young woman to come in during the days while he attended his grandmother at night. That didn't work out well, so a woman was hired to live in to care for the house and Granny. She was an older woman, experienced with elderly people. This was a positive and workable solution for them. Jim and his father had considered a nursing home, but neither felt that would be best. The expense of hiring the live-in woman was no greater than nursing home expenses would have been, and Granny was able to remain in her home and have personal care.

Another friend, Shirley, was an only child, so the caregiving responsibilities fell to her. When her father's crippling arthritis forced her parents to give up their Arizona home, they bought a mobile home close to Shirley. She cared for their basic needs much as I had cared for my folks' needs.

After her father's death, her mother lived alone. When multiple heart problems and colon cancer surgery resulted in cardiac arrest, it was obvious that Shirley's mom couldn't take care of herself. Shirley's options were to sell the mobile home and move her mother to a nursing home, or to move her in with their family. They decided to sell the mobile home and use the money to build an addition to their house. The addition consisted of a living room, a bedroom and a large, convenient bath. Her mother joined the family for meals. It gave her the privacy of a place of her own, yet she enjoyed the security of being with her family.

Shirley's mom was able to stay by herself while Shirley worked as a teacher's aide, until she began to show signs of Alzheimer's disease. Then Shirley hired "Home Care Givers" to come in while she worked. This solution worked best for Shirley's situation.

While everything worked out fine for Shirley's mom, her Aunt Laura was another story. Aunt Laura was in her nineties when it became clear that she could no longer live alone. She needed daily care, but Shirley couldn't take her into her home. As a result, they evaluated nursing homes and chose one. Shirley cared for her aunt's financial situation and visited her regularly, always keeping in touch with her needs. However, Aunt Laura didn't accept the move willingly or graciously.

I understood how Shirley felt because I had been in the same situation with my grandmother. She couldn't live with my aging parents, so I found a care facility in Nanny's hometown where she had grown up. I thought she would be happy there and have the enjoyment of memories and people she knew. Unfortunately, it was quite a distance from my home and my folks' home. We couldn't visit her often, and we learned that she was desperately unhappy.

I then located a care facility near our home, and Nanny lived there until we moved her into our three-bedroom, one-bath home. She lived with us from November until April. She didn't have her own room but we gave her a room at the end of the hall that had an open staircase and was close to the bathroom.

There was no privacy for her or us. By April I felt ready for a mental institution. I was trying to care for my parents' needs, my in-laws' needs, Nanny's needs, as well as the needs of my own family. I prayed for a workable solution.

Finally, we were able to move Nanny to a care facility in the town where she had lived and where my folks still lived. It was a beautiful and well-run facility. However, she became ill and had to be hospitalized, so she had to be moved again.

We located another nursing home, quite a distance from our homes. We had no other choice. She was not happy to be away from her home or my folks, and I felt sad about placing her there, but my aging parents and my own family were priorities. She was well cared for and lived into her ninety-fifth year.

Not every decision you'll have to make will be a popular one. When illness and infirmities strike your loved ones, you may be forced to make some hurtful choices. It is difficult to tear people away from their homes. You'll probably feel guilty or misunderstood or even angry for being put in such a position.

I'd like to encourage you at this point. Sometimes you have to make tough decisions. But just remember to encircle the choices you make in love and prayer. What works for one person may not work for another—and that's okay. Only you and those in your situation will be able to decide what will work best.

Reevaluate Solutions as Circumstances Change

One of our weightiest decisions came when my folks could no longer stay at the farm during the hard winter months of New Hampshire. I drove out there every day on ice-covered roads and then shoveled snow. It was too much for me, but I worried that my father would fall on the icy driveway going to the mailbox. Then my mother's arthritis became too painful to bear the frigid winters in a drafty, too-big farmhouse. Eventually we decided to seek a retirement village in Florida where they could remain independent yet receive care.

We located an apartment within their financial means and to their liking. It was in a quad with caring and watchful neighbors, and with a chapel, shopping area and medical facilities close by. The level ground made slow-paced walking easy. Oak trees spread their shady branches, and in nearby fields cattle grazed with egrets perched on their backs.

My folks were happy with the decision and as enthusiastic as children about their new winter home. We shopped for the first new furnishings they had ever owned. Mom was pleased with her white and gold French provincial bedroom furnishings and the high-backed, yellow floral chair.

It was an ideal arrangement. They looked forward to a social life with close neighbors that they had not enjoyed at the farm, and they could be outside more of the time since Mom's arthritis was eased by the warmth. In November I helped them pack and flew with them to Florida to get them settled. After I returned home, we talked often on the telephone and through letters, and my brothers and sisters visited them several times.

When spring returned to New England, my father was eager to get back to the farm. I flew to Florida to bring them home. During the summer months I continued my daily trips to the farm to care for their needs. This arrangement worked well until the third year when Mom had a severe allergic reaction to a cortisone shot only weeks before they were to leave for their winter home. She developed large painful sores on her body and couldn't raise her arms even to feed herself. Her memory was also affected. I didn't know what to do. I couldn't stay at the farm, yet my home wasn't adequate for their needs.

My brother Ken and his wife, Phil, came to the rescue. Ken had a busy veterinary practice so he was unable to stay at the farm, but Phil came prepared to stay as long as necessary. For several weeks she cooked for my folks, cleaned house and cared for their daily needs, while I drove out every day to bathe Mom and dress her sores.

We debated the advisability of their going back to Florida when Mom recovered. Where would be the best place for them under the circumstances? We discussed the warmth of Florida where they would have the convenience and comfort of their little apartment as opposed to a difficult winter in New Hampshire. Mom and Dad chose to return to Florida.

I was uneasy about them being so far from any of the family, but I arranged for a nurse to visit daily to give medications and care for physical needs. Others would clean the apartment every week and bring in meals each day. When I felt I had covered every need, I left for home, driving to the airport with a heavy heart. I wondered what other arrangements I should have made. Later I returned to the apartment for something I'd forgotten, and I found both Mom and Pop weeping. It still hurts to think of that time.

During the winter they did well and were cheered by family visits. I kept in close touch by telephone. On May 3 a neighbor called to say Mom had had congestive heart failure and was in intensive care. I called my sister Bren to make flight arrangements for me, threw a few things into a suitcase, and said a hurried goodbye to my husband. Friends drove me almost a hundred miles to the airport in Boston. I arrived just in time to see the plane pulling away from the terminal. I threw down my suitcase in total despair, sure that Mom would die before I could get to her. But Bren took control and got me on another flight leaving immediately.

The flight had a layover of several hours in Miami, and I realized as I sat waiting in the airport that that time was a gift from the Lord. I was able to think and pray, to call upon God's grace before facing the difficult situation ahead.

Sam and Edna, my folks' neighbors, met me at the plane in Orlando. My dear father was also waiting for me, tears streaming down his face. "I knew you'd come," was all he could say as he hugged me.

Mom was in an oxygen tent, still in intensive care, and wasn't aware that I was coming. When she saw me she said in a surprised whisper, "My angel."

I had no way of knowing if I would be in Florida a few days or a week. It depended on whether Mom lived through this attack...and then...what? She began to recover slowly and we visited her every day in the hospital. Even with her progress we could see that it was going to be a long haul for all of us.

I had no idea what to do. It was obvious that the days of their living independently on the farm were gone. I prayed for guidance, for answers, for a plan. But the days were like blank sheets of paper. As I walked to the chapel one day I could offer nothing more than, "Help, Lord."

I was frustrated and lonely. My husband was in New Hampshire. My children were traveling somewhere between Oregon and Alaska. And every day, in his halting garbled way, Pop would ask, "What are we going to do?"

Making the Best of Your Situation

After almost two weeks in Florida I was standing in the kitchen door wondering what was coming next when a tiny voice in my mind said, "God doesn't really hear you, and He doesn't care." This jolted me out of my thoughtfulness and I said, "Yes, He does. He said He will never leave me nor forsake me." I knew God would answer; I just didn't know when or how, but I hoped it would be soon.

It was my birthday and I cried as I talked with my husband in New Hampshire. But his words encouraged me. He said, "As long as you have to be there, enjoy the sunshine. Buy some shorts, get a good book, and try to relax. I'm doing fine and I love you." That was good to hear. My father came out of the bedroom and handed me a little red box with a rubber band around it. It was his birthday present to me, a collection of pennies he had been saving for a long time—$6.23.

I was ashamed for my shortness with him, for expressing my displeasure at having to be there when I wanted to be home. What I had to learn about love!

I followed my husband's suggestion and tried to relax and read, trusting that the Lord would answer my prayers for help. Then one day my sister Glo called. "It's about time we got you home," she said. I couldn't have agreed more. She and I discussed the possibility of a nursing home until another arrangement could be made. We didn't like the idea, but it was the only practical solution at the time and under the circumstances. Both Mom and Pop agreed so Glo set the wheels in motion and located a place near her home.

We knew it was their last winter in their Florida apartment, the end of living independently. My brother Ken flew down to accompany them and get them settled in the nursing home. Bren met them at the airport in Boston. My other brother, Bob, flew to Florida with his son to rent a truck and bring back their belongings. My family's help was God's answer to my prayers.

On June 3, just a month after I left New Hampshire, I stood alone in my parents' empty Florida apartment. I wandered around with the memories of those weeks echoing in my mind and heart. Another phase in the progress of time and of age had come and gone. I closed the door.

———

When caring for an aging loved one, you'll find yourself having to make choices that you wish didn't have to be made. Remember that God does care and He's ready to listen.

When faced with decisions:

- Make them ahead of time with your aging loved ones and family if possible.
- Determine your needs for your particular situation.
- List your options.
- Choose the option that is in the best interest of your loved ones and the caregiver.
- Don't make choices in haste or out of guilt.
- Pray about every decision. God is your best resource.
- Reevaluate as circumstances change.

PART I

The Feelings

3

Recognizing Your Feelings

When my folks arrived at the nursing home in New Hampshire, my mother was still weak from her attack of congestive heart failure. As usual, they decided to explore their new surroundings, and typical of her independent spirit, Mom took her walker instead of letting my father push her in the wheelchair. She overextended herself and her health began to fail rapidly.

When my sister visited them, she found my mother in bed, crumpled, uncomfortable and in pain. She spoke to the head nurse about my mother's condition, and the nurse said, "Gloria, your mother is going to die, and we won't take any heroic measures."

"Yes, I know she's going to die," my sister replied, "but she is my mother and she has the right to die with dignity. And she will, or I'll know the reason why."

My mother was old and sick. The professionals who cared for her did not see her as the beautiful woman, loyal wife, mother of seven or artist that she had been during her life. They did not know the stories she could tell.

During this time I was learning God's ways, but I didn't understand His love. How could He allow such indignity in the lives of His children? I was angry at nurses and doctors who saw only the oldness and could not see the young, dynamic, independent and hard-working individuals these people once were. Why couldn't they see my loved ones not as worn out and useless, but as wise from their years of experience? I wanted others to see the value and the significance of these lives.

It wasn't just the nursing home staff who seemed to disregard those who were helpless and infirm. On one cold winter day, we waited in a doctor's office long past our appointment time. My mother and father were tired and hungry and uncomfortable from sitting so long. I wanted to take them home where they could eat and rest in comfort. The doctor was too overbooked to honor their appointment time.

I was angry to the point of tears at the very fact of age. Age meant being at the mercy of inconsiderate people who didn't care about the old, and I felt helpless to change it.

One time I told a young doctor about my mother's severe allergy to cortisone. The doctor ignored both my statement and my mother's. "Of course you're not allergic to cortisone," he said. "No one is allergic to cortisone," and he proceeded to inject both her knees. The reaction caused large open sores on her arms, affected her memory and led to disorientation.

Society's Feelings Toward Old Age

Unfortunately, those attitudes about age and the elderly are all too common. We live in a society where aging people are rejected as having no value because they've ceased to be "producers." A person's value is equated with his or her production level. Paul Tournier, in *Learn to Grow Old*, says it well:

> We have given things priority over persons, we have built up a civilization based on things rather than persons. Old people are discounted because they are purely and simply persons, whose only value is as persons, and not as producers any more.[1]

With new medical discoveries and improved health care, society now has more elderly than ever before. The only problem is, society doesn't know what to do with these people. Erik Erikson, in *Vital Involvement in Old Age,* says:

> In a country that has prided itself on independence rather than interdependence, on fresh zest and enthusiasm rather than cautious deliberation, and on agility and buoyancy rather than forthright firmness, the predominant value is, of course, youthfulness ... It is not surprising, then, that ageism poses such a problem for all older people. Young is beautiful. Old is ugly. This attitude stems from a stereotyping deeply ingrained in our culture and in our economy. After all, we throw old things away—they are too difficult to mend. New ones are more desirable and up-to-date, incorporating the latest know-how. Old things are obsolete, valueless and disposable.[2]

We have only to look at the latest styles of clothing, the most recent ad campaigns, the current songs on the radio or movies in the theater to see who society caters to. There is an unspoken prejudice in our society that doesn't allow people to grow old. *Growing Old in America* illustrates this attitude:

> Prejudice against the aged—ageism—is manifested in several ways. American society is obsessed with youth ... The media, once accused of showing the elderly as ineffectual and unattractive, has now concentrated on showing extraordinary achievements of the aged, rather than portraying their ordinary, often satisfying lives ... Cultures such as ours with urbanization, industrialization, and increased mobility have reduced the significance ... and lowered the regard for old age ... One strong element of our attitudes toward the elderly and toward becoming old is the economic valuation of human work. How much a man makes, how large his house is, etc., is important in determining personal worth in this society ... At the same time, the society holds them in less esteem because they are

no longer "productively" contributing to the community.[3]

We can give our aging loved ones value by our acceptance and love. Yet if you're like me, you realize that we can fail in giving them that value by resenting their helpless dependence, their intrusion into our lives, and the interruption of our plans. Perhaps you're finding it difficult to accept what is happening and the uncertainty of the years of your obligation. I would encourage you to embrace your situation as given by God. Only then will you be able to accept and love those who cause the disruption.

When Angry Feelings Surface

I had not learned this when we moved Nanny into our home. She thoroughly disrupted our household. To be honest, at first I didn't mind. I even felt a little virtuous about caring for my grandmother.

But it was only while she was ill that I cared for her willingly. When she began to recover, I became resentful. I was angry that at ninety-two she still had good health while both my parents had young spirits trapped in pain-racked bodies. My anger affected both my attitude and care. I wouldn't include Nanny in our family dinners or in any family affairs. She was partial to my niece who lived with us and unkind to my daughter, and I struggled with that. I felt trapped by the situation, but I was actually trapped by my feelings of anger.

I was emotionally unprepared to care for my grandmother. If I had recognized my feelings of anger and dealt with them, forgiving her and responding with God's love, her life would have been more pleasant, and certainly my family and I would have had happier memories of the months she lived with us.

Are you angry? Have you thought how your anger is aggravating your situation? Seek ways to deal with your anger. (We'll talk about that more in the next chapter.)

Unresolved Feelings From Past Hurts

Sometimes our anger may stem from forgotten hurts of the past that surface with the responsibility of caregiving.

After Nanny's death, I was confronted by the offenses I had suffered because of her that had lain dormant since childhood. The bitter feelings I felt manifested themselves when I was in the emotional pressure cooker of caring for her.

For years Nanny was unkind to my mother and caused many problems in the family. Worst of all, she was abusive to my baby sister whom I loved dearly. I had never before faced up to those feelings. When I understood the source of those feelings, I had to ask God's forgiveness for my anger *and* my unkindness toward my grandmother. I also had to forgive Nanny so those offenses would never again be a source of bitterness and complaint.

Do not begin your responsibilities as a caregiver with unresolved problems and feelings because they will eventually manifest themselves. Aged loved ones become prime targets for unresolved anger, fear or guilt. This opens the way for emotional, verbal and physical abuse.

If you do have unresolved feelings toward your aging loved one, find someone to talk to about it, whether it be a pastor, a counselor or an insightful friend. You'll be surprised at the burden that will be lifted once you deal with these feelings.

Common Guilt Feelings

Guilt is like a thorny branch that pricks us wherever we turn. We feel inadequate; we can never do enough or be good enough. Guilt drives us to keep going even though we are burned out, to overcompensate for our shortcomings according to our evaluation of ourselves. It allows us to be manipulated and dominated.

Betty, in a tired voice, told me her mother demanded that she come to her house every day, even though the older woman was still in good health and able to work in her small garden. When I suggested a companion or housekeeper, Betty said, "Oh, Mom won't let anyone in the house except me."

Betty felt guilty because she couldn't cope with a full-time job, a husband and home, and her mother's demands too. She felt that since she was the daughter, it was her responsibility to do as she was told, harkening back to her childhood days. Her mother was pulling the strings according to what she wanted with no consideration for her daughter.

"Why do you feel guilty?" I asked.

"I feel guilty," she said, "about my anger and rebellion, and my feelings toward my mother. I feel guilty because my mother can no longer function as well because of her age."

Betty carried the burden of her mother's age. Even though her mother was able to live in her own home, she took advantage of Betty's guilt and her sense of duty by not allowing her to live a normal, peaceful life. Betty needed to come to grips with her feelings and to deal with the guilt and other emotions that were leading to emotional and physical exhaustion. She needed to take control of her own life.

Can you relate to Betty? Are you overwhelmed at times with guilt? Edwin Kiester, Jr., in "Stretched to the Limit," calls this situation "The Guilt Trap." He says:

> Many already frazzled caregivers suffer an additional burden of guilt, borne from a deep feeling of obligation to their parents. The sandwicher's refrain is, "She took care of me when I was a baby, now it's my turn to take care of her." Another common self-justification is, "People took care of their families in the old days ... and we always take care of our own."

He quotes from gerontologist Elaine Brody:

> Both these ideas are based on myths and prevent harried caregivers from seeking help or attending properly to their own needs.[4]

Dona felt guilty when she went out for a social time with friends. Her mother lives with her and is a semi-invalid. She is a cheerful and deeply spiritual woman who encourages Dona and doesn't use self-pitying remarks to make Dona feel guilty. But Dona feels guilty anyway because she is able to be independent while her mother is confined to her chair, unable any longer to control her own life.

You're probably dealing with feelings of guilt—whether the guilt is deserved or not. Why don't you take a few moments to write down what you feel guilty about? As you look over your list, decide which things you can change and which things you cannot change. Do you need to ask anyone's forgiveness about your real guilt feelings? We'll address the issue of dealing with guilt more thoroughly in the next chapter.

Emotional Exhaustion

Anger, grief, frustration, helplessness and guilt all merge, and the result is emotional exhaustion. We try to make up for what our loved ones have lost. We try to assuage our guilt by overcompensating, giving in to every demand, never considering our own needs. We still behave as children; they still act as parents.

Exhaustion is often more emotional than physical because of the tension, the uncertainty and the decisions. We are dealing with the lives of those we love, and we become enmeshed in emotions that drain the energy from us.

I had reached the point of exhaustion from trying to keep up with the demands of home and family as well as making the long drive to my folks' home every day. When I expressed my tiredness to my husband, his suggestion was that I stay home for a day to rest and relax.

"I can't. They need me," was my reply.

But my husband wisely said, "This is not from the Lord. You're doing this to yourself." And then he added, "Your mother would probably be happy to know that you're going to be at home resting today."

He was right. I was driven by my guilt and the feeling that they couldn't or shouldn't be alone to fend for themselves. He was right, too, about my folks. They were relieved that I was going to have a day of rest.

If we understand our own feelings about ourselves and about aging, and if we recognize the feelings of our older loved ones, we will gain perspectives that will help us to see old age as a valuable time of life. We, as well as society, can learn and grow from these insights. By confronting our feelings and attitudes, we will be better equipped to deal with the increasing problems and dependency of our parents and grandparents.

The caregiving trail is a long one. There are no easy answers or clear-cut solutions. The relationship of adult children, who are themselves on the fringe of old age, with their aging loved ones, who are living out their last stages of life, is fraught with complex emotions. These feelings cannot be dealt with once and for all, but if we learn to recognize them and deal with them as they arise, using God's resources, we can make those last years happier for our loved ones and for ourselves.

———

Take an inventory of the feelings you experience because of your situation. We can recognize our feelings when we catch ourselves:

- Reacting with abusive behavior—emotionally, verbally, physically.
- Neglecting our priorities. Our life is out of balance.
- Over-extending ourselves and ignoring our limitations.
- Refusing to take care of our own personal, physical and emotional needs.

4

Dealing With the Feelings

D uring the years I cared for my loved ones, I struggled and prayed, feeling helpless, panicky, exhausted, frustrated, angry and then guilty because of these feelings. I wanted to get on with my life as I wanted it to be, but I realized that would happen only when my loved ones died.

If only I had learned to deal with my feelings earlier, to be kinder, more patient and not so angry, the blessings would have been multiplied many times over. I could have rejoiced with my parents at each step of progress instead of scolding them for taking a chance. And I could have struggled less and prayed more.

We all have our "if onlys," but it is not wise to spend a lot of time on them. We must make the best of what we have and go on with life and, in the process, encourage others. Helping others recognize the importance of dealing with emotions can turn our stumbling blocks into stepping stones and more lives will be blessed.

Facing Negative Feelings

We have the ability to experience love and happiness, but also anger, frustration, grief and guilt. Negative feelings are not sinful. It's what we do with them that makes the difference. How should we deal with these emotions that cause

turmoil and ungodly attitudes and actions? Unless we recognize and acknowledge them, and do something about
them, they stay inside and torture us. Emotions pop up in
the middle of the night when we can't sleep and they
interrupt our time with the Lord. If we are experiencing
anger, grief or depression, we need to remember that hiding
feelings, or trying to, does not make them disappear. They
will reveal themselves in some way, usually unpleasant, as
mine did with my grandmother. It does not do any good to
deny that we feel anger and pass it off as frustration or
impatience. The root feeling is still anger.

Anger with my father and his stroke condition showed
itself in little unkind ways. I insisted that he clean his own
dentures, and he tried. But his hands were clumsy and he
couldn't hold the brush with his afflicted right hand. It was
such a small matter. Why couldn't I be gracious and kind?
I was angry with his helplessness and with myself for my
unloving spirit.

It is hard to admit that we are angry with our loved ones.
After all, they are our parents and we love them. Acknowledging the anger doesn't make us more angry or less, but it
does clarify our thinking and it is a beginning of the relief
needed.

Journalizing

One of the ways I came to terms with my feelings was to
"journalize." My notebook was my private outlet. Instead of
continuing along in my endless state, I was able to verbalize
my emotions. Usually I directed these notes to God.

One of my journal entries reads: "Oh, Lord, I'm angry,
and I'm tired—so tired that I don't want to get up. I feel
terrible and I look terrible. I hate the thought of getting old!
I hate the thought of my folks being old. I don't know if I'm
doing the right thing for Mom and Pop. Help me, Lord."

One of the wonderful things about God is that He isn't
shocked by our words. My daughter said to me once, "It

really is a relief to know that God is big enough to handle my actions." Whether the words were on paper or in my mind, He knew they existed—but it helped me to express them.

Praying

Besides expressing ourselves in a journal, we can express our feelings to God in prayer. His Word says, "In everything by prayer and supplication with thanksgiving let your requests be made known to God" (Philippians 4:6, NASB).

Praying about our emotions is not just a trite answer. God is our greatest resource, and He not only cares about our feelings, but He also feels them with us. We are not talking into the air but to the God whose Spirit lives within us. Who would know the feelings of our infirmities better than He? (Hebrews 4:15) He knows how we feel and why, and He also knows how to bring relief through the Scriptures. The Bible promises that if we are obedient to His Word, we will have love, peace, joy, patience, kindness, goodness, faithfulness, gentleness and self-control (Galatians 5:22, NASB). These are the antitheses of anger, fear, guilt and helplessness. God gives us guidelines to help us deal with those feelings.

The Thanksgiving Principle

One of God's first guidelines for me was to give thanks in everything (1 Thessalonians 5:18). It is hard to give thanks when everything is in confusion and we don't feel thankful. But He did not say when or if we *feel* thankful. True thankfulness comes from knowing that we have a God who controls our lives and circumstances, who is sovereign, and who is able and willing to go through it all with us.

Sometimes God has to get us on our knees before we get the message, and that's where I was when I learned my first lesson in "giving thanks in everything."

I had fixed Nanny a tray of creamed chicken and peas and a cup of hot tea. Just as I set the tray on her lap, a sudden movement upset the tray (I always suspected it was the Lord). Nanny's lunch was in her lap. The peas rolled off the tray, down the blankets and under the bed.

I was on my hands and knees, with my head under the bed, rolling peas into the dustpan when the still small voice of God reminded me of a decision I had made only the day before. The theme of a book I had been reading was based on the above verse in Thessalonians: "In everything give thanks, for this is the will of God in Christ Jesus concerning you." I had to make a decision. Would I give thanks or not? I decided to see if it "worked" as the author said.

I asked, "Now, Lord?" It didn't seem appropriate, but God said, "Now." Still on my knees, with the blankets over my head, I muttered, "Thank You, Lord." I felt a little foolish as I said it, but instantly my thoughts changed from grumbling and turned to God Himself. As I cleaned up the peas and tea and chicken, and my shocked grandmother, I felt the joy of the Lord.

From then on I worked on the Thanksgiving Principle, and a new spirit of joy and praise began to replace the angry attitudes that had been with me so long.

What happens when we give thanks in a bad situation? The negative thoughts are turned *away from* the situation and *toward* God; *away from* the downward pull of grumbling, bitterness and anger *toward* positive thinking. Even if we don't understand the reasons, God knows what effect this has on our minds and, consequently, on our behavior. It is an acknowledgment that God is aware of our needs at that very time, and it helps us to trust Him.

The verse previous to this gives another basic principle: to pray without ceasing (1 Thessalonians 5:17). Giving thanks in everything helps us develop an awareness of God and it becomes a habit to converse with Him at any time. We don't have to be on our knees or in the closet. He is with us on the freeways, at stop lights, in the grocery store—He never leaves us. When we are aware of God at all times, we know we can communicate with Him through His Spirit within us. We begin to live in His presence.

Hanging on to God's Word

I became a committed Christian only months before the caregiving responsibilities began. When everything was changing and I was confused, God's Word became the only stable thing in my life. I talked to God all the time. One day I talked, or rather cried, to God when I was nearly at the end of my rope. Tears dripped off my face into the soapy dish-water.

It was a cold, windy March day, and the kids were packing for a basketball tournament in Maine. There was general confusion in the house, and Nanny was roaming around, probably wondering what kind of a nuthouse she was in. It seemed like weeks since I'd been out of the house and free of caregiving jobs.

Then the septic tank backed up. In a one-bathroom house with four teens, an elderly grandmother, and Wayne and me, that was bad news. My husband and son had pipes apart in the cellar and were snaking to the septic tank, which they couldn't locate under three feet of snow. And the smell...

I was hanging on to the Lord's hand as tight as I could, but I felt as if another hand was around my feet pulling me down, and my nose was barely above water.

The telephone rang for the hundredth time. It was a friend asking if I would be a chaperone for the kids going to Maine. Would I? My husband said, "Go." He was willing to take care of Nanny so I could get away for a day. That night in Maine it started to snow. The snow turned to a blizzard, and before the games were over the roads were closed. We couldn't go home! After the games we all met in the church for a rally, and there we bedded down for the night. The kids sang and the adults talked, but I couldn't do either. I went to the altar and curled up before God, praying and resting.

Morning came and the sun shone bright on a brittle day. Snow was piled higher than the cars, but the roads were open. Several hours later as I rounded the sharp curve on the steep hill toward home, the car slid off the road and buried itself in a snowdrift. We struggled the rest of the way through blowing snow and cold.

At home nothing had changed. Nanny was totally confused; the house was a disaster and smelled like the septic tank had moved indoors; and the problem had not been solved. But I was different.

I read in Hebrews 12:11:

> All discipline for the moment seems not to be joyful, but sorrowful; yet to those who have been trained by it, afterwards it yields the peaceful fruit of righteousness (NASB).

My situation was not joyful and I felt as if I were in boot camp, but I began to comprehend that there was a purpose in it all and that there was an "afterwards."

God understood my problems, and He gave me a snowstorm in which to renew my strength so I could cope.

A Renewed Mind

Larry Crabb in *Basic Principles of Biblical Counseling* says,

> A renewed mind is one which renews the belief that was held at the point of salvation: God is totally sufficient for me.[1]

If God is aware of our feelings, and we know He is, we know we can trust Him to have some answers to our feelings, and that He is sufficient to help us cope.

God's Word speaks about anger, fear and guilt. Whenever I became fearful that I wasn't making the right choice for my folks, I reminded myself of 2 Timothy 1:7: "For God has not given us the spirit of fear, but of power and love and a sound mind" (KJV).

Philippians 4:6, quoted earlier, goes on to say that "the peace of God will keep your hearts and minds in Christ Jesus." These verses and others reminded me of God's sufficiency and my dependency on Him. Choosing verses that speak to our emotions and placing them where we will be reminded of them keeps our minds fixed on God, rather than on ourselves. They remind us that He is our strength and our sufficiency in our weaknesses.

When He renews our minds, He changes the pattern of our thinking. It is then up to us to change our behavior. When we don't feel loving or thankful, we can feed our minds with that which will transform our attitudes. God's Word gives us the practical solutions we need, as well as the consequences of unbridled emotions.

The twenty miles from my folks' house was tedious during the summer because of tourists. Slow-moving sight-seers dominated the single-lane country road. I picked my husband up at work every day, and he didn't like it when I was late. But I often worked at my folks' home until the last minute and allowed myself barely enough time to get to his workplace. My anger and frustration would build as I tailed a sightseer. Soon I would mutter (and worse). When finally I could pass the car in front of me, my feelings would be obvious to its driver. My attitude and behavior did not please God, I'm sure.

One day God caught my attention with verses about renewing my mind, having the mind of Jesus, giving thanks in everything and praying without ceasing. I knew I would have to change my ways. It was up to me, not God, to decide how. Since it was my responsibility to pick up my husband on time after a long day with my folks, I disciplined myself to leave earlier. When I was slowed by tourists and moving at twenty-five miles an hour, I began to memorize Scripture instead of raising my blood pressure. I was amazed how much more relaxing the drive became, and I managed to arrive on time and keep my husband happy too.

Yes, God is our greatest resource. We can never over-estimate His power in dealing with our feelings.

Dealing With Guilt

Is there any feeling more insidious than guilt? It affects our whole person. Edwin Kiester, Jr., in his article "Stretched to the Limit" says, "Of all the burdens that sandwich families carry, all agree that guilt is the heaviest."[2]

We set standards for ourselves because of our feelings of obligation, because we have an unnatural authority over our loved ones, and because we want to replace what they have lost. Then we cannot live up to our standards. Spiritually, this keeps us from enjoying close communication with God. We feel unworthy. Emotionally, guilt dogs our steps and gives us no peace of mind. Physically, it drains and exhausts us. You've probably asked yourself how to cope with this guilt that plagues you. Will it ever go away?

There are two kinds of guilt we must deal with: true guilt that involves sin and interferes with our relationship with God; and false guilt that we carry within us and that involves our emotions and self-concept.

True guilt is from God, urging us to repentance. It is not a burden causing us to berate ourselves into feeling useless and inadequate, but it is an inner sadness for our sinful condition before God. The Bible gives us the remedy for true guilt in 1 John 1:9:

> If we confess our sins, He is faithful and righteous to forgive us our sins and to cleanse us from all un-righteousness (NASB).

False guilt is like a millstone around our necks con-tinually pulling us down. It plagues our minds, affording us no rest or peace. False guilt concentrates on self with all its weaknesses and failures, constantly punishing us with re-criminations and accusations.

When we recognize whether our guilt is true or false, we can begin to deal with it. However, even knowing what God says, sometimes we continue to feel the weight. It helps to ask ourselves some questions and answer them honestly:

- Am I doing everything I can to make my loved one comfortable?

- Am I showing respect and kindness?

- Am I caring for my family properly, not giving them the "leftovers"?

- Am I trusting God with the caregiving responsibilities and accepting my task as from Him?

- Am I caring for my own personal needs so I will not burn out before the task is finished?

- Is my guilt the result of sin, a wrong committed against God that must be made right? Or is it a feeling about myself and my attitudes?

Our feelings are not sinful. Sometimes guilt is an emotional response to what we *think* is sin. But God says,

> Beloved, if our heart does not condemn us, we have confidence before God; and whatever we ask we receive from Him, because we keep His commandments and do the things that are pleasing in His sight (1 John 3:21,22, NASB).

If we have confessed our sins to God, we have His promise that we are forgiven. Any guilt left over is from "the accuser of the brethren" and not from God.

Forgiving Ourselves

If our answers are honestly acceptable to ourselves, and we are giving it our best, then we must forgive ourselves. How? **First,** by remembering that Satan is the accuser of the brethren. He is the one who makes us feel inadequate. "Resist the devil and He will flee from you" (James 4:7, KJV). Concentrate on God's forgiveness and His peace.

Second, by renewing our minds through the Scriptures. God's Word has transforming power. **Third,** by thinking on the positive things accomplished instead of what isn't being done. We can give ourselves a few strokes. We need them— we deserve them. And **fourth**, we need to keep our sense of humor and not take ourselves so seriously. Laugh a little— laugh a lot.

If the answers to the bulleted questions above are negative, now is the time to make some positive changes in attitudes and behavior, and not flail ourselves with false guilt or weaknesses.

The "guilties" are not going to disappear overnight. They will continue to crop up at the most unexpected times. Satan is not going to let us off easy. Even though it's been years since my folks died, the guilt still sneaks in once in a while, and I remember the times I was impatient or unkind or angry. It makes me feel sad and uncomfortable and have the "if onlys," but I remember that I have been forgiven for my blunders by God. I am free from guilt and my heart does not condemn me.

Accepting Help From Other People

God has made us to help each other. We need to talk about our feelings with someone who cares or who is experiencing the same caregiving problems. Sometimes we feel guilty expressing our feelings, particularly the negative ones, because we don't think Christians should have them. We are often our own harshest judges. Those who have been through similar experiences will understand and become our greatest encouragers.

Seek out a support group of caregivers. Many times a church or community will know of a group you can contact. If there is not one in your church or area, pray that the Lord will bring people into your life who have or have had the same problems. It is easy to feel that you are the only one struggling. Perhaps you feel others will think you less spiritual, and you feel guilty, thinking that if you were more spiritual, you wouldn't feel the way you do. Feelings are not an indicator of spirituality. How they are dealt with is the indicator of spiritual strength and trust.

Members of a support group can encourage and strengthen each other through their understanding and availability, and through their faithful prayers.

Dealing With Long-Standing Feelings

Many feelings that we deal with are long-standing. They began in childhood and stem from early influences in our lives. Dr. Clyde Narramore, in his lecture *Understanding Why I Feel and Act the Way I Do*, describes them by three overlapping circles. He concludes that man is three-part: emotional, physical and spiritual. If any one of these is out of balance, we do not function to our best capacity.

The feelings and problems that plague you may have their roots in childhood, or you may have taken up reproaches against your aged one as I did against my grandmother. If you cannot work through them, seek professional help from a Christian counselor.

Forgiving Others

Going a step further in dealing with our feelings, God has instructed us to forgive others as He has forgiven us. Forgiveness is a freeing agent both for us and for the one we forgive. When I forgave my grandmother for her unkindness, it was no longer a sore spot in my life or an issue of complaint. God was allowed, by my obedience, to further conform me to His image.

God has programmed life with stages of growth and maturity. From infancy to old age, each stage of life is unique, and none is more valuable in God's sight than another. Only society places superficial value on a particular stage. How we grow and develop from one stage to another will depend on seeing ourselves and our aging loved ones from God's perspective, understanding and dealing with our own feelings, and accepting each responsibility as it is entrusted to us by God.

━━━

To be more effective in your role as caregiver, you'll need to face your feelings. When dealing with your feelings:

- Acknowledge your feelings. Face the fact of them.
- Define your feelings—anger, true or false guilt, etc.
- Identify the source of your feelings—physical causes, childhood, circumstances, unrealized expectations.
- Journalize your feelings.
- Pray about your feelings.
- Talk with a support person or counselor. Get professional help if necessary.
- Learn to respond according to God's principles as given in the Bible.

5

Recognizing Your Parents' Feelings

A geriatric nurse who had cared for elderly people for twenty years wrote the following "make-believe" letter to Ann Landers. She said that "it could have been written by any one of dozens of people that I have cared for."

Dear Caregiver (wife, husband, son, daughter, brother, sister):

I'm sorry you have to go through all this unpleasantness every day, and I regret that I am the cause of it. I hate not being able to do so many things for myself. It's awful to be totally dependent on someone else.

I feel ashamed that I can't go to the bathroom on my own. It's frustrating to be fed by another person. I'm absolutely disgusted that I am unable to get a tissue up to my face so I can blow my nose. Being old and helpless is much worse than any illness or disability. It does things to one's feelings of personal worth.

Worst of all is knowing how you hate being my caregiver. I see the resentment in your eyes and I hear it in your voice. I know that deep down you wish I would die and get it over with so you can get on with your life and not be bothered with me.

Well, I wish the same. Surprised? I have no choice, however, but to live out the years that have been allotted to me. I'm sorry that the job of caring for me has fallen on your shoulders. I wonder which of us carries the bigger burden.[1]

This letter sums up many of the feelings the aged experience. The body gets old and infirm but the person's spirit and soul don't age. The feelings are still there. And the losses are great—to be old and helpless, at the mercy of whoever happens to become the caregiver, is the utmost in humiliation. Losing the ability and strength to do even the smallest intimate things, the ones we take for granted, reduces a person's self-worth. They see it coming and there is nothing they can do but try to accept their plight with grace.

Dependency

My mother loved to walk to the barn and sit in the big sunny doorway for a time of quiet devotion and prayer. After she got arthritis, she was no longer able to get to her most precious spot. It was a sad loss to her.

She had been a strong woman, extraordinarily so, until her forties when the arthritis began to affect her joints. Her knees became swollen and painful. Her hands and wrists stiffened, her fingers grew knobby and clumsy.

The years went by and she became more dependent on me because she would lose her balance and fall. I had to help her into the bathtub or shower, then dry her and help her dress. How humbling it must have been to be exposed and helpless before her daughter.

As Mom aged, the pain began to show on her face and every step took its toll on her heart. Only minutes after she died, a weight was lifted from my chest, and I realized that for years I had breathed for her with every painful step.

My father's illness affected him in a different way. Whenever I took him downtown, he saw friends and townspeople he had lived and worked with all his life, those he had served as Selectman, and he would be unable to communicate even the simplest sentences. Often he would begin to cry, embarrassing himself and those he was attempting to communicate with.

There are many losses, and each one takes its toll on the self-respect and independence of our loved ones. I took my independent, social mother-in-law downtown to get her driver's license, but the examiner refused to renew it. It was terrible to witness her realization that she would no longer be able to attend her social functions, grocery shop, or even drive downtown to lunch on her own. My vivacious mother-in-law aged in her humiliating dependence.

Guilt

Whether aged ones suffer physical loss or the loss of independence, there is bound to be lowered self-worth. These losses place them in situations where they are dependent on their adult children. The children, often not prepared to be caregivers, become impatient with the role, and our loved ones then have to cope with the guilt of being burdensome.

There is hardly a deeper guilt than having to sit by while another person feeds, washes and dresses you, and cleans your house, all the simple acts you have done for a lifetime. This is how the aged feel. They realize that they are adding problems to the life of their child, or the one caring for them, and constantly apologize for being burdens. They know it isn't going to get easier.

When I went to care for my folks, I often took my weariness and frustration with me. I became impatient or frustrated easily, and this caused my mother to fret because of my tiredness. Consequently, she felt guilty thinking she and Pop were the cause of it. I didn't realize how great the burden was that I inflicted on them.

Several years after my folks died, I was in an accident. Lying helpless in a hospital bed, I was dependent on nurses and my daughter for feeding and washing me, brushing my teeth, and other intimate care. I felt humiliated, but also guilty because of the added burden placed on my daughter. She willingly and lovingly cared for me and was never impatient or unkind, but I felt I was robbing her of time and strength that could have been directed in other ways. I was frustrated because of my limitations.

Have you noticed your aging loved ones expressing guilt feelings? Perhaps you've thought of a way to help ease their worry. We'll discuss this further in the next chapter.

Ridicule

When we begin to get lines and wrinkles in our faces, we experience a sort of panic. If our knees don't work as well as they did, or when it comes time for bifocals or trifocals, we grumble and complain. As people age they lose their physical attractiveness; their bodies don't function well; they don't see or hear as clearly. There's nothing to reassure them because they are losing on every side. And as if the losses weren't enough, stooped and wrinkled women and men are often ridiculed by the young.

I was walking behind an elderly couple not long ago. They were little people holding hands as they walked along talking to each other. A young woman on a bicycle watched them and signaled with her eyes to her friend. Those signals ridiculed them; she was laughing at them. I felt protective and wanted to defend them from the lack of respect.

Fear

Along with the humiliation, frustration and the grief of loss, the aged feel helpless. They have lost control of their lives. While I was praying and pondering on the solution to our care problems in Florida, my father anxiously asked several times a day what we were going to do. I could only answer that we would "wait and see what the Lord reveals." His anxiety stemmed from his helplessness to put any kind of plan into operation. All his life he had been in control of situations, making plans and decisions. He was a man of action.

Out of this helplessness comes fear: "What's going to happen to us? What if we run out of money? Who will take care of us? Who is going to make the decisions?" Knowing they cannot function normally and being totally dependent on someone else increases their feelings of low self-esteem and anger at what they have become.

Aging loved ones fear losing their mental capabilities. This is a very real fear as indicated by the many times one hears the elderly say, "I don't mind growing old as long as I have my mind."

Some of us have seen people with Alzheimer's disease or other mental disorders, and the consequent lack of control and independence. Erikson says, "In its most profound sense...mental disability seems to loom as a shameful helplessness that will permit no vestiges of autonomy, in the realm either of behavior or of internal feelings."[2]

Another fear of the elderly is being victimized by crime. According to Irwin I. Kimmelman, Attorney General for the New Jersey Department of Law and Safety, it is not the number of crimes, but the

> terrible and tragic impact that crime has on [the elderly] that is significant. Crime simply causes much more fear among the elderly and has a far more deleterious [harmful] impact on the quality of their lives.

> Even so-called non-violent crimes such as purse snatching, vandalism and burglary can be devastating. Stolen or damaged articles and property are often irreplaceable, either because of sentimental or monetary value.[3]

Kimmelman goes on to say that once the elderly are victimized, they may "become obsessed with the idea that they will be victimized again...They may develop a very negative outlook on life and even alter their lifestyle, as they resort to extreme precautionary measures."[4]

An elderly friend of mine was attacked and robbed, beaten and knocked unconscious. When he regained consciousness, he dragged himself to the telephone and called for help. Although he was hurt physically, the emotional damage was greater. He retells his experience often, asking for prayer, and he has a fearful attitude even though his faith in God is strong. Recovery and healing are slow in coming to my friend.

Fear of death looms over the heads of every elderly person. The reality of death is not somewhere in the future, something that will never happen to them. It is imminent. Death is an unknown, a lonely time. It has to be faced alone. A strong and continuous faith in God and the hope of eternity with Him keeps them looking beyond the actual dying. But death is still a fearful curiosity.

Losses

Life for the aged is filled with losses. When persons reach the age of ninety, most of their friends and loved ones have died. They are alone in a world that has little tolerance for loneliness, helplessness and dependence. Losing a faithful husband or wife, a companion of many years, can be a devastating blow to the elderly. It is like being deserted, rejected, to have that one you have loved and depended on for years leave at the time when he or she is needed most. The depression that results from this grief can cause physical and mental problems.

Considering the backgrounds, temperaments and influences of the aged ones, we can expect varied reactions to old age and infirmity. There may be a stubbornness that insists upon autonomy, denying the reality of age. For some there will be woeful self-pity that demands inordinate attention. But the key to caregiving is to understand who the aged ones are, who they have been during their lives, and what they are going through as they necessarily, but reluctantly, relinquish more and more of themselves to age.

When we begin to understand the emotions of our aged loved ones, to realize what a difficult time of life it is for them, and when we understand our own feelings and emotions, we will become more sensitive to them. Caring for the elderly is a difficult job, but being elderly isn't easy either.

———

The person you're caring for is a human being first. Recognize the feelings of your loved ones by:

- Learning to see and understand from their point of view.

- Responding to your loved ones with love. They are special to God.

- Accepting your responsibility as given by God. Do it heartily as unto Him.

6

Dealing With Your Parents' Feelings

The Florida weather turned very hot and humid during the month I stayed with my mom and dad. We could find no shade anywhere. My father reacted with huffs and puffs and desperate declarations of the heat. I tried to persuade him to stay inside and remain quiet, and to "think cool" because his agitated body and mind aggravated the condition. However, his mind was on the heat and nothing could deter him.

My mother, on the other hand, was content to sit quietly, surrounded by letter-writing materials and books. The perspiration trickled down her face and her hair clung in damp wisps on her forehead, but she didn't complain.

What made my two parents react in such different ways to the same situation? As I reflect, I realize that it was natural for them to react as they did because they were of opposite personalities.

Each of us is born with a basic temperament. Florence Littauer in her book *Personality Plus* compares the temperaments with Michelangelo choosing the basic material for his statue of David:

> He knew he could change the shape of the stone, but he couldn't transform the basic ingredient... We were all born with our own temperament traits, our raw materials, our own kind of rock... Our type of rock

doesn't change, but our shapes can be altered ... Our
circumstances, IQ, nationality, economics, environment, and parental influence can mold our personalities, but the rock underneath remains the same.[1]

According to studies, there are four basic temperaments: the strong choleric, the happy sanguine, the
thoughtful melancholy, and the quiet phlegmatic. Each of
these has character traits identifying that particular temperament. Most people have a blend of traits—such as san-
guine/choleric or phlegmatic/melancholy—with one being
stronger than the other.

It isn't my intention to go into depth about the temperaments here. Florence Littauer and others have already done
this. However, it is important to have an awareness of the
temperaments in order to know ourselves, understand
others and improve the quality of our relationships. In
dealing with the feelings of our loved ones, we begin by
understanding their basic temperaments.

Understanding the Personality Traits

My father had a strong choleric temperament with many
sanguine traits. He was strong-willed and stubborn, out-
spoken and adventurous, but he was also unsympathetic,
impatient, domineering and intolerant. However, he loved to
laugh and have fun. In his younger days he took part in
plays and minstrel shows. He was a baseball player, a
drummer and a dancer. It was he who played Santa Claus
to the many town children at the annual Community Christmas Tree.

Mom was peace-loving and went to great lengths to
smooth any rough waters. She hid her emotions and didn't
react to my father's outbursts and moods except to com-
ment, "Now, Ken, don't get all worked up." She had a
phlegmatic temperament and sanguine traits that had become submerged as the stress of child-rearing, the pain of
arthritis and the weight of financial burdens bore down

upon her in her middle years. I remember when she went about her work whistling cheerily, but that ceased when the constant pain in her body began.

The sanguine is the extrovert and optimist. He likes people and likes to be the center of attention. Fun-loving and talkative, when the gaiety ceases, sanguines become depressed.

The choleric is an extrovert who gets things done, usually his way, and he is an optimist. The word "impossible" only challenges the choleric. He has strong leadership qualities and it is natural for him to take control. However, when cholerics lose control of their lives or have to relinquish control to another, they become depressed.

The melancholy is an introvert and a pessimist. He is a perfectionist, likes everything neat, and is deep and thoughtful, artistic and moody. For those who like to have everything around them orderly and efficient, the loss of these qualities causes depression.

The phlegmatic is peace-loving, an introvert and a pessimist. He seldom shares deep emotional needs and has little understanding of those who do. The phlegmatic is not one to get involved, yet he has administrative talents because of his ability to get along with people. The phlegmatic is a live-and-let-live person. When the life of the phlegmatic loses peace and quiet, and there are drastic changes, he becomes depressed.

What Happens When Temperaments Clash

When we attempt to see our loved ones in terms of their temperaments, and try to understand what they have lost or how their lives have changed, we can recognize some of the causes of their feelings.

While I was caring for my parents, I knew nothing about the different temperaments—either mine or theirs. My sanguine/choleric temperament often clashed with Pop's. I was as strong-willed and stubborn as he was.

After his stroke, I was certain that he would be restored to his former activities if he just tried hard enough, and I pushed him. One day he wanted to send postcards to friends back home. I insisted he write the cards himself, stating emphatically that he could do it if he would only try. He reacted to my bossiness and impatience with stubbornness and tears. He had lost control of his life and nothing could restore that control.

I also reacted to the low-key, non-responsive temperament of my mother. After her serious congestive heart failure, I was afraid that if she exerted herself she would have another attack.

I had to be away one day and insisted that she not leave her wheelchair unless she first called a neighbor. When I returned, the neighbor was there—Mom had attempted something beyond her strength. I was angry and Mom cried, which she didn't often do in front of anyone. She felt bad because she had disappointed me. I would have felt better if she had put me in my place and reminded me that I was still her daughter. She had been used to going about her life with no fuss or fanfare, but now that had changed and she had lost her independence.

What are the conflicts with your aging loved one? Is it in part due to a clashing of temperaments? It is important that caregivers recognize the temperaments of their loved ones to understand who they are and why they act the way they do. If I had been aware of my parents' temperaments, and my own, perhaps I would have responded differently. We need to accept others with their own unique personalities and not expect our loved ones to respond to situations the way we do.

Paul Tournier, in his book *The Healing of Persons*, says,

> The reason for our study of the temperaments is that we may learn better to know ourselves and what God wants of us. It is in order to submit and consecrate our temperaments to God, for him to use in accordance with his purpose.[2]

As we submit our temperaments to God, He will help us overcome our weaknesses and use our strengths wisely. Knowing our temperament is not an excuse for unkind or unacceptable behavior on our part. Like Michelangelo's marble, though the material always remains the same, the shape can be changed through the power of the Holy Spirit.

Responding to the Feelings of the Aging

The more we learn and understand God's responses, the more effectively we can deal with the feelings of our loved ones and affirm their value as persons.

As our loved ones become more infirm and more dependent, they begin to feel useless and of no value. They experience guilt for the excessive burdens placed on their loved ones, usually their children. They need affirmation that they have significance.

Now that her knees have became so painful, Dona's mother feels useless. She is unable to help Dona with small household chores. At times in the night she can't manage to get from her bed to the bathroom without her daughter's help. She feels worthless to Dona who works hard as a fifth-grade teacher.

But Dona won't accept those expressions of uselessness, and wisely and lovingly affirms her mother by telling her how helpful it is to talk and be listened to after a day at school. She appreciates being able to bounce ideas around with her mom, and values her opinion. Dona assures her by letting her know that she depends on her mother's daily prayers and spiritual strength. Physically the caregiving is difficult and exhausting, but Dona's affirmative attitude continues to build her mother's self-worth.

Affirmation is a scriptural principle according to Hebrews 10:24: "Let us consider how to stimulate one another to love and good works . . . encouraging one another" (NASB). We need to practice this principle in our caregiving.

Kindness is like a rare jewel, shining into the life of others. Some of its facets are tenderness, thoughtfulness and compassion. Kindness is unselfish and gracious. I have a precious son-in-law, and if I were to use one word to describe him it would be kind.

People need and respond to kindness. When we are caring for our loved ones it is an important quality to have —to be forgetful of self and conscious of the needs of others.

I began to learn kindness during my caregiving years. Sometimes it means just doing little things for the comfort of another. Those acts don't seem important to us and yet they are remembered by the recipient.

The nights in Florida were chilly after the hot days, and my mother would be sweaty and uncomfortable. It was difficult to get her in and out of the bathtub, but after I gave her a bath and a soothing back rub and smoothed and warmed her sheets with her electric mattress warmer, she would sigh with contentment and fall asleep within minutes. It was a pleasure to care for her in that way, to see her comfortable and relaxed following a pain-filled day.

Kindness is an attitude of the heart and it reflects our love for others and our love for God.

The meaning of love has become perverted, weak and mawkish, having more to do with physical characteristics than strength of character. Actually, real love is powerful—it stands when everything else is crumbling.

Love is very patient and kind, never jealous or envious, never boastful or proud, never haughty or selfish or rude. Love does not demand its own way. It is not irritable or touchy. It does not hold grudges and will hardly even notice when others do it wrong. It is never glad about injustice, but rejoices when the truth wins out. If you love someone you will be loyal to him no matter what the cost. You will always believe in him, expect the best of him, and always stand your ground in defending him ... Let love be your greatest aim (1 Corinthians 13:4–7; 14:1a, TLB).

These qualities don't come without effort. We have to will to love, to make love a commitment, not a sentimental attachment to an idea. Once we will to love someone, the practice begins: to be patient when we are tempted to be impatient, to be unselfish when we find ourselves giving more than we want to give, to be kind when we are tempted to be hateful. When we begin to exercise the *elements* of love, even though we don't have the *feelings* of love, God honors our obedience and brings the feelings in the form of fruit, the fruit of the Spirit: love, joy, peace, patience, kindness, goodness, faithfulness, gentleness, self-control (Galatians 5:22, 23, NASB).

My mother and father were fine examples to me of this love. They continued to love me even when I was impatient or selfish or proud. They never ceased to be concerned for my well-being.

I hadn't yet learned God's way of loving others during the early years of caregiving, and my desire was strong to be certain that my folks knew Jesus Christ. One day I was trying to persuade my father to "accept Jesus as your Savior" but my method was imperious, without tenderness and humility. It didn't work, of course, and I found myself once again impatient. There was so much pride and arrogance in me.

Later, my mother said to me, "The only way to win him is with love." She had loved my father with patience and unselfishness. She was never rude or arrogant, nor was she ever boastful or jealous. She was loyal to her core. The love I should have been lavishing on them I was yet to learn from my mother.

In the beginning, especially, caregiving isn't easy. It is demanding and exhausting. Perhaps your loved ones are the hateful, proud and angry ones, but God says that love never fails. We are the winners when we love the way God expects us to love. It not only changes the hearts of those we are learning to love, but our own hearts as well.

An important aspect of that love is forgiveness. Many times we harbor anger and bitterness against our loved ones from our childhood as I did with my grandmother. Forgiveness means setting aside our pride, an action that is unnatural and uncomfortable. But we must forgive as we have been forgiven and clear the slate for the adventure of loving.

Do you feel the need to forgive someone? I encourage you, through prayer, to deal with this issue. It will be a constant hindrance in your relationship with those you care for until you do.

Dealing with our parents' feelings begins with discerning their feelings, understanding their loss, and not letting our own emotional disposition control our responses. Our loved ones need to express their feelings, and we need to listen, to hear what is behind their words. What comes out as anger is often a manifestation of a deeper emotion.

By learning to respond to our aging loved ones' emotional needs and not react out of our own needs, we can give them back their sense of significance. We all know how important it is to be listened to and how rejected and humiliated we feel when someone turns away before we have finished what we were saying. In *Caring For Your Aging Parents*, Barbara Deane calls this active listening:

> As we learn to listen with our hearts as well as with our ears, we become more godly people. "Active listening" is another name for this.

> Active listening will help you to break the habit of responding predictably when your parent pushes one of your hot buttons. It can help you to break out of the circular communications trap that so many families are in—going round and round about the same old things.[3]

If we become aware of the temperaments in order to relate to our parents more effectively, if we learn to listen and then practice God's responses of affirmation, kindness, love and forgiveness, our relationship with our parents will be revitalized and blessed.

———

Are you beginning to see your situation from your parents' point of view? Are you taking a peek through their eyes? We can learn to deal with our parents' feelings by:

- Understanding their feelings
- Listening with understanding hearts
- Becoming aware of the four basic temperaments, better understanding why we think and act as we do
- Affirming our parents to give them a sense of value
- Practicing kindness
- Forgiving our loved ones for past wrongs; asking forgiveness for our past wrongs to them
- Practicing God's responses, the characteristics of love as found in 1 Corinthians 13

PART II

The Facts

7

Knowing the Physical Needs

A s I talked with people taking care of their aging loved ones, over and over I heard, "I never thought of my parents getting old," and, "It happened before we were ready for it." You probably feel that way too. You were probably caught a bit off-guard. I know I was. Despite the fact that age doesn't come suddenly, very few are prepared for the reality of it.

Changes happen with increasing speed as the years go by. And nothing happens more noticeably than the physical changes of age. Eyesight dims, hearing diminishes, endurance lessens and muscles slacken. You'll be better able to care for your parents and loved ones if you prepare for the physical needs that result from aging. We'll talk about how you can address those needs in this chapter.

Medical Problems

As our loved ones age and we begin even the most basic care, we need to be aware of their existing medical problems, the medication they are taking and the doctor(s) treating them.

Often we are not aware of medications being administered, but these drugs may contribute to conditions that might not otherwise exist. We blame the condition on physical or mental causes rather than getting to the true cause—incorrect medication.

My sister, who has taken care of several relatives, feels it is very important to be aware of any medication an older person is taking, and to observe the effects of that medication. She says, "Medications are such an important issue with the sick and elderly. Dan's mother was given some kind of medication when she had been in the nursing home a short time. She started to hallucinate and became very agitated. Then she went into angry rages where her strength was so great that she was almost uncontrollable. As soon as the medication was regulated, she calmed down.

"The same thing happened to Dan's brother in the hospital. He hallucinated, lost his power to communicate and went into a nearly vegetative state. Having had the experience with his mother, we inquired about the medication and requested that it be stopped. Within a day or two he returned to normal. Had we not known about this, he may have lain in his hospital bed for days or weeks with us thinking he was ready to die. The doctors did think that. Although he lived only two and a half weeks after that episode, he died alert and able to communicate with us to within the last day."

Sometimes medications can cause a person to become lethargic and unresponsive. Dona's mother was in the rehabilitation hospital following surgery and a slight stroke. After several days Dona noticed her lack of responsiveness, dull eyes and slack mouth. That was very unlike her. Dona took her home and got her into a regular routine again and within a short time she was responding in her normal enthusiastic way.

Hearing Problems

Barbara McDevitt, Case Manager for the Community Outreach Program for the Deaf in Tucson, Arizona, says that aging people tend to neglect their hearing, many times denying that a problem exists. Caregivers can suspect a hearing loss when the aging one talks louder, turns up the volume on the radio or television or moves closer to the television set, or doesn't respond to the telephone or door-bell.

McDevitt works with the hearing impaired and counsels with caregivers who face the hearing loss of their loved ones. She said it is especially frustrating for caregivers when loved ones are reluctant to admit their problem or wear a hearing aid.

According to McDevitt, those who are losing their hearing often become withdrawn because they can't hear what is being said and are embarrassed to ask someone to repeat it. This embarrassment causes the hearing-impaired to avoid conversation, and thus become isolated from social contact, which in turn creates depression and lowers self-esteem.

Hearing loss is usually gradual with the onset of age. However, poor health can emphasize the loss. McDevitt said that those who exercise, stay active and continue to care for their health generally will have better hearing than those who are inactive.

What can caregivers do to help their loved ones cope with hearing loss? Adjustments will be necessary, and some positive things can be done to keep your loved ones inde-pendent and help them maintain their dignity.

- Talk with your loved one about the hearing loss and its effects on him (or her) socially, physically and psychologically. Assure him that the loss doesn't af-fect your love and care or his value.

- Have him examined by a certified audiologist. Be careful of those who offer discount hearing aids and free examinations. Follow the specialist's recommen-dations for a hearing device.

- Help to keep your loved one independent by making changes in his home. For example, a doorbell that switches on a light will get his attention.

- When awakening a deaf person, or attempting to attract his attention, flick a light switch. McDevitt stated emphatically that one should never tap a deaf person to awaken him or get his attention.

Many devices are available for the hearing impaired. Hearing aids can help, but you need to understand that it is not the same as natural hearing. Hearing aids do not screen out surrounding noises as does the natural ear.

Hearing aids are not the only alternative. There are special telephones for the deaf that enable the person to perform tasks such as order theater tickets, make airline reservations and communicate with friends. Because the phone is portable, those who suffer from hearing loss can be more independent than ever before.

There are many other types of assistance available. Universities and teaching hospitals are excellent sources of information. Check your telephone book for programs designed for the deaf and hearing impaired. If they are unable to help, they can refer you to someone who can. Many organizations for the deaf are local, but United Way is available across the country.

Eyesight Problems

Vision loss is another serious problem often brought on by age. Problems with eyesight should be properly cared for by qualified eye specialists. Perhaps the eye condition could be corrected by surgery. A talk with the eye doctor will give you information that will make your job easier.

Jon Miller, Executive Director of the Tucson Association for the Blind and Visually Impaired, said that 15 percent of adults begin to lose their vision after age sixty-five, and the loss increases with age. Macular degeneration is the leading cause of visual impairment. It is a gradual process where peripheral vision remains, but the person is unable to read, drive or recognize people.

Miller emphasized the need for regular visual examinations since many eye diseases can be treated if discovered in the early stages. Cataracts and glaucoma are two such treatable diseases.

According to Miller, vision is the primary sensory input and vision loss brings psychological consequences. Again, the aging ones lose their independence and may become angry, frustrated or depressed. Caregivers can help by making the necessary adjustments as uncomplicated as possible.

One of the skills that will need to be learned by a visually impaired person is that of eating. The caregiver can help with that adjustment by placing food on a plate by the "clock method." That is, certain foods are placed in the same position as hands on a clock. Potatoes may be in the one o'clock position with vegetables at three o'clock and meat at six o'clock. This method gives the blind person some security and it facilitates the eating process.

Other skills such as pouring coffee can be relearned also. As difficult as the task may seem to be, the visually impaired person will do well if he or she asks for assistance.

Safety is an important factor as well. Caregivers need to be aware that falls and burns are common among the visually impaired. Stove knobs can be identified and flame arresters installed so a wrong turn won't result in a burn or a fire. Medications with identifiable labels, placed where the person can easily reach and distinguish them, will assure that the wrong medication won't be taken.

Miller pointed out that, sadly enough, many motorists are uncaring of the visually impaired. Walking on crowded or uneven sidewalks or crossing streets with lights must be learned and caution exercised.

Caregivers can help their loved ones remain independent by showing them a new way to cook and by monitoring their diets. They can shop for nutritional food that is easy to prepare and easily identified.

Consistency is important. The blind person is "walking in the dark," so furniture and other objects should remain in the same place. Tripping or bumping into things can cause not only confusion and disorientation but injury.

If your aging loved one cannot see, medical problems such as sores, blisters or bruises might develop unnoticed. Caregivers must be alert to these potential problems. Hygiene and cleanliness are often neglected because the aging one cannot find the soap, deodorant, lotion or toothpaste. These should be easily identifiable and placed in the same location after each use.

Clothing can be marked with Braille tags for identification. Clothes also can be arranged by color grouping or in other creative ways so the blind person can dress with ease and be coordinated.

It is important that you, as a caregiver, understand the disability, and that you encourage and teach independence. It may be difficult for you not to take over for your loved ones who are struggling, but as you seek guidance and assistance, your job will be much more rewarding.

And please remember your visually impaired loved ones are not deaf or mute. They can speak for themselves, and they can hear when people speak in normal tones.

According to Miller, a device called the "vision simulator" simulates the condition of the visually impaired person, and it helps those with sight to realize the handicaps of their loved ones. The Tucson Association for the Blind and Visually Impaired encourages families to work together and to use this as well as other resources available to them.

Dental Problems

Many times as people get older dentures don't fit properly, causing discomfort as well as hindering proper chewing of food. Sometimes loose or ill-fitting dentures also make speaking difficult, which is humiliating to the older person. Proper dental care will give your loved one security in social situations and assure better health.

The more knowledgeable we are as caregivers about these problems, the more we will be able to help our parents live quality lives. Talking with doctors periodically and getting their evaluation of our parents' condition will help us keep current in our care methods. It will also keep us informed of any medication changes. This will, at the same time, reassure our loved ones and free them from unnecessary anxieties.

Knowing the Facts About Strokes

Many times unexpected problems arise over which we have no control. This was the case with my father's stroke. I was unaware of his blood pressure problem. He was healthy and strong, active physically and mentally. My mother badgered him about having a physical checkup, but he was headstrong and refused to keep the doctor appointments she made for him. Unfortunately, a condition that may have been avoided by medication caused years of distress for him, my mother and our family.

There is a fine line between interfering in the lives of our loved ones and being helpful in the beginning stages of caregiving. It takes wisdom and loving discernment to know when and how to step in.

When my father became ill, I had no idea how to deal with a stroke victim. I wanted him to regain his former vigor and youthfulness. Consequently, my expectations were unrealistic, and frustration was the result for both my father and me. As a caregiver, I should have taken the time to learn the basic facts about stroke patients, so I could have been more objective in my evaluation and expectations. If I had, I would have realized that those who have suffered strokes cry easily and become discouraged and depressed. They experience deep grief from their loss of physical, mental and social functions.

Symptoms of Stroke

The American Heart Association has published a booklet for families who are caring for stroke victims. "Strokes: A Guide for the Family" includes warning signs and symptoms by which we can recognize the condition:

- A sudden weakness or numbness of face, arm or leg on one side of the body
- Loss of speech, or trouble talking or understanding speech
- Sudden dimness or loss of vision, particularly in one eye
- Sudden unexplained headaches, or a sudden change in the pattern of headaches
- Unexplained dizziness, unsteadiness or sudden falls, especially when associated with any of the symptoms listed above[1]

Help for the Caregiver

Caregivers are often at a loss when they have to care for a stroke victim. Along with their own grief, they have to deal with the psychological and physical consequences of the stroke in their loved one. The American Heart Association is a willing helper for caregivers. The following suggestions are found in the booklet mentioned above:

- Divide duties so the full burden of care doesn't fall on one family member. Accept help from friends who volunteer. Friends often want to help but need a family member to tell them how.
- Help the recovering person take responsibility for exercising regularly.
- Gradually and easily let the recovering person assume responsibility for self-care and other activities. This calls for fine judgment to encourage independence but not promote unrealistic expectations. If she can brush her hair or dress herself, let her do so even if it takes a long time.

- Praise any successful effort, and don't be discouraged by failures. Recovering from stroke is a slow process.

- Have the recovering person participate in as much family planning as he or she can. Feeling useful is a tremendous morale booster.

- Help the recovering person stay in contact with the world. Don't push him to the sidelines and trust the television and radio to fill the time. Encourage him to develop a hobby. Spend time together; perhaps playing chess, checkers or bridge could be fun. Encourage people to visit if the person's condition warrants it. Make the recovering person feel wanted and a part of the social picture.

- Check with the doctor regularly. And call if things aren't going the way you think they should.

Further information on stroke victims and their care can be obtained from The National Stroke Association at (303) 762-9922.

"Senility"

While stroke victims can be helped through therapy, there is nothing that can be done for the irreversible brain damage sometimes caused by a stroke. A more common mental condition in the aged that often can be helped is lumped under the name of "senility." This accounts for everything from misplacing keys to forgetting a person's name.

According to *Growing Old in America*:

> Senility . . . is not a normal sign of aging, nor is it even a disease. The symptoms of what is popularly called "senility" include serious forgetfulness, confusion, and numerous other personality and behavioral changes.

> Emotional problems that are more common among the elderly, such as boredom, loss of self-esteem, depression that follows the death of friends and spouses, are

often mistakenly confused with irreversible brain damage.

Mental decline in old age may be called "dementia," "organic brain disorder," "chronic brain syndrome," "arteriosclerosis," "cerebral atrophy," or "pseudodementia." What is important is that some of the problems that fall under the medical description of "senile dementia" can be treated and cured while others can only be treated without hope of restoring lost brain function.[2]

Alzheimer's Disease

One of the diseases of the mind that is currently incurable is Alzheimer's disease. It is a progressive mental disease that has been described as a "thief of the mind" because it insidiously destroys brain cells, causing subtle and persistent changes in behavior and attitude. It quite literally robs the victim of his personhood. Researchers feel they are getting closer to solving the problem but as yet there is no conclusive evidence of the cause.

Symptoms to watch for, according to the fact sheet from the Alzheimer's Association, include "gradual memory loss, decline in ability to perform routine tasks, impairment of judgment, disorientation, personality change, difficulty in learning and loss of language skills."

This helpful fact sheet on Alzheimer's disease and related disorders can be obtained by writing to the Alzheimer's Association, 16787 Bernardo Center Dr. #8, San Diego, CA 92128, or by calling (619) 295-2509.

Linda Demkovich, in an article titled "The Brain Game," quotes Dr. Robert Butler, director of Mt. Sinai Medical Center:

Beyond drugs, some patients can be helped by extra caring. By keeping them in a "protected social environment, in which they are fed and otherwise cared for," they may still be able to go out into the community and function in a relatively normal fashion.[3]

While standing in line at a cafeteria one day, I noticed a striking elderly couple behind me. He was a dignified-looking man with white hair and a white mustache. He was impeccably dressed in a white suit and white broad-brimmed hat, the personification of the Southern gentleman. Beside him, holding his arm, was a lady dressed just as impeccably in a scarlet dress adorned with tasteful silver jewelry. Her white hair curled softly around her face, and her green eyes sparkled. The only thing out of place was that she didn't wear dentures. They were an outstanding looking couple.

I spoke to them, expressing how lovely they looked together. The lady smiled and made some reply. They were both eighty-five years old, the gentleman told me. Then, in a low voice, the gentleman added, "She's an Alzheimer's victim, but we've been together for sixty years, and I love her."

I wanted to hug them and thank them for the beautiful example they were. It was obvious to me that the husband was protecting and caring for his beloved wife as tenderly as if she were his new bride. He gave her respect and dignity in her unfortunate condition.

For the caregiver, dealing with Alzheimer's is a heartbreaking and exhausting task. To watch a loved one begin that slow deterioration and slide into total mental degeneration is difficult emotionally and physically. Patients may initially be cared for at home, but as the disease progresses and constant watchcare is required, it may be necessary to admit them to a nursing facility, preferably one that specializes in Alzheimer's disease.

A friend whose husband died with this disease after ten years told me that it was heart-wrenching to place him in a home. She had cared for him until he began to leave the house and remove mail from mail boxes. She never knew

what he would do next, and it became impossible to leave
him unattended while she worked.

Others told of afflicted loved ones turning burners on to
heat water and forgetting about them, endangering themselves and the household; another dialed the telephone not
knowing who or where she was dialing.

There are many sad stories of loved ones being victimized by Alzheimer's disease, and there is pain and grief
as caregivers watch helplessly while their loved ones slowly
become another, unknown person.

To help caregivers, there are support groups affiliated
with the Alzheimer's Disease and Related Disorders Association (ADRDA). These groups share the common tragic bond
of loved ones with Alzheimer's disease, and the purpose of
the group is to share and help each other cope with their
circumstances and emotions. If there is no support group in
your area, write to ADRDA, P.O. Box 99037, San Diego, CA
92109, or call (619) 295-2509. They can give you information on starting a chapter in your area.

Being Prepared

It is important for caregivers to have some knowledge about
stroke and Alzheimer's disease, cardiovascular diseases,
diabetes and arthritis as well as other diseases that strike
the elderly.

If your loved ones are manifesting strange or unfamiliar
physical or mental symptoms, contact a doctor and have
them tested and evaluated. You may want to get a second
opinion to validate the findings.

Learn as much as possible about the condition—its
symptoms, progression, prognosis, expectations and limitations. Find out about diet and exercise, therapy and medication. The more knowledgeable you are, the greater the
chances of keeping your loved ones in the best possible
physical and emotional condition.

This knowledge combined with the love and strength of Jesus Christ will give you coping power as it is needed, and after the death of your loved ones, you will be blessed for the time and love you gave.

———

Dealing with the physical changes brought on by old age is a difficult task. Do what you can to understand these changes and when you review the facts:

- Become knowledgeable about diseases common to the elderly.
- Learn symptoms, prognosis, expectations, limitations, therapy methods, medications.
- Learn about your loved ones' dental, visual, medical and medication needs.
- Consult with doctors on your loved ones' condition and evaluate their needs.
- Use the many valuable resources available to help with your task.
- Combine your knowledge and methods with the love and strength of Jesus Christ for coping and caring.

8

Knowing the Housing Needs

Their Home or Yours

My friend's ninety-six-year-old mother lived in a rather dangerous neighborhood in Los Angeles. In excellent health, she loved her home, and her joy was her routine of arising early to have breakfast, tidying the house and keeping closets and cupboards orderly. She knew her neighbors and the neighborhood, and she did not live in fear for herself. She was adamant about remaining in her own place. Her daughter, however, wanted to move the mother out of her home and into a care home.

What is the best decision in this situation? If the mother is uprooted from her lifelong situation while she is doing well, and forced to live in a room with few or none of her personal belongings, having no daily tasks or responsibilities, is this the best for her?

I have tried to put myself in the position of both the mother and daughter. How would I feel if I had lived in my home for a lifetime, was healthy and felt secure? From my perspective I would want to remain there as independently and for as long as possible. If I became ill or unable to care for my own needs, and no live-in or daily help was available, then would be the time to move me into a care facility.

On the other hand, as the daughter, I would be concerned for my mother's welfare. What if she should fall, or
be robbed or mugged in that undesirable neighborhood?

The choices often depend on our feelings. If the caregiver
feels guilty about not caring for her aging loved one, or is
unable to meet the basic needs of grocery shopping, laundry
and cleaning, she might feel better having her mother in a
care facility. That could relieve the guilt and anxiety. However, if she sees the situation from her mother's point of
view, she will allow her mother to live out her life as long as
possible, independently, in her own home.

Not long ago my friend's mother suffered from congestive
heart failure. She was in the hospital until her condition
stabilized. It was then she realized she could not live alone
without help, and she was admitted to a care facility. This
relieved the daughter from making the decision to take her
mother from her home against her will.

Aging ones are sometimes at the mercy of their caregivers. It may be necessary to make a heart-rending decision
regardless of the strong feelings of attachment the loved
ones have to their home. But the situation of those loved
ones should be carefully considered and evaluated, and the
choice must be based on what is best for them, not on the
guilt or anxiety of the caregiver. To keep an aging loved one
as independent as possible for as long as possible may mean
finding creative ways to meet their needs.

Preventing Falls

According to an article by Robin Marantz Henig,

> Falls are the second leading cause of accidental death
> among women between sixty-five and eighty-four, and
> the fourth leading cause of accidental death among
> men in that age range. For people over eighty-five, falls
> outrank all other accidents as a cause of death.[1]

Henig states that falls occur because of drugs and
medication, the natural aging process of degeneration of

bone and muscle, and balance abnormalities. These physical causes can be eased or perhaps avoided by reviewing the safety of the home. Usually when loved ones continue to live in their own homes, we may overlook factors that they have lived with all their lives such as rugs that can be tripped over, high or uneven doorsills, bathrooms with no handrails or with no protective anti-slip mats in tubs or showers, and poorly lighted areas that become more unsafe with failing vision.

My mother's arthritis caused her knees to stiffen. She walked slowly, almost shuffling. Her balance was poor. She also suffered from osteoporosis, and every fall resulted in a broken or fractured bone.

One day Mom walked to the front hall of their home and opened the heavy door. The wind caught it, pushing her backwards. She lost her balance and fell, causing a hairline fracture in her hip. Another day while visiting my brother's home, she tripped over a throw rug and dislocated her shoulder. Still another time she lost her balance and fell over one of her grandchildren, down two steps, and landed on her arm and face breaking her elbow and her glasses.

I learned to go before her to clear any obstacles, whether rugs or grandchildren, and to realize that what was no problem to me could be a danger to her.

If we look at the home from an aged person's perspective, asking ourselves the following questions, we can see where the trouble spots are.

In the kitchen:

- Are cupboard doors within reach and easy to open?

- Are utensils where they can be found without fumbling in a drawer? Are they separated from sharp objects?

- Are the stove knobs within reach, and is the oven door manageable?

- Does the floor have a non-slip covering?

- Is there adequate lighting, and a continuous light for nighttime?
- Is it necessary for the aged one to bend down to retrieve a pan hidden in a cupboard?

In the bathroom:

- Do they have to step into the tub to take a shower, causing a problem for stiff joints and poor balance?
- Are there handrails to hold onto, and are they securely attached and in the best locations?
- Are there anti-slip decals in tub and shower?
- Is the shower curtain secure and out of the way to avoid tripping or tangling?
- Do shower doors operate smoothly to avoid getting locked in the shower or causing confusion in operating?
- Are hot and cold water clearly indicated and the fixtures easy to operate?
- Is the commode the proper height with a well-secured seat?
- Is the lighting adequate?
- Is the floor covered with anti-slip material with no loose edges to cause tripping?
- Are medicine cabinets at proper height, easy to open, with adequate lighting?
- Are door locks simple to operate?
- Are light switches handy?

Go through the house and remove any rugs, loose tiles or corners that could trip an unsteady person. Check for sharp corners on tables, and doorsills that are too high for shuffling feet. Check for lamps that clumsy, arthritic hands could tip over and for lamp cords that could entangle and trip. Remove any stools that would be a temptation to climb on. The secret is to anticipate the danger spots so that falls, burns, cuts and bruises can be minimized or avoided.

When the safety check is complete and the home is as hazard-free as possible, and if the loved ones are in reasonable—if limited—health, encourage them and allow them to enjoy their independence.

If they are to remain in their own home, it may be necessary to hire part-time help, utilize services of a nurse, or employ a live-in caregiver. The caregiver could be a companion-housekeeper, and may be required to do unskilled nursing care such as changing diapers if the loved one becomes incontinent.

When Jim and his dad had to make a decision about Jim's grandmother, she had lived independently for many years. However, at this time her condition necessitated constant care. The choices were to place her in a care facility or keep her in her home and hire a live-in caregiver. They decided to keep her at home and began the task of finding a competent person to give the care.

They looked for several important characteristics in the caregiver: a person who understood and liked elderly people; someone who had good health and stamina; a person with a patient and loving spirit; a person who was orderly and clean in personal habits. They also required someone who could bathe, dress and feed their elderly one. It could become necessary for the caregiver to lift and turn the grandmother, and to change diapers and soiled bed linens.

Not all caregivers have all the desirable characteristics you want for your loved one. However, if the situation can be monitored closely and no abuse is suffered by the aged one either physically or mentally, it is worth the effort to know that he (or she) ended his days in dear and familiar surroundings.

After Jim's grandmother died, it was agreed that the choice to keep her at home had been the best for all concerned.

Despite the many falls my mother suffered, we struggled to keep her and my father independent until the last month of their lives. It was demanding and exhausting and there was much anxiety, but they maintained the privacy of their relationship in an atmosphere of comfort and familiarity.

My daughter, Lori, was a live-in caregiver for a woman in her eighties. She said, "Taking care of Mrs. S. was one of the most delightful things I've done."

Lori stayed at the home of Mrs. S. from Sunday evening through Wednesday evening when another caregiver came to stay the remainder of the week. It was twenty-four-hour care, being on hand should Mrs. S. need anything. She said the things that made her duties pleasant were that Mrs. S. took care of herself, wearing attractive dresses, make-up and jewelry. She also had a routine for her day.

When I asked Lori about her own responsibilities, she gave me an overview of her day. She was Mrs. S.'s helper and did light housekeeping. She prepared meals attractively, putting flowers or little things on the tray or table that would bring pleasure to Mrs. S. Lori drove her to church, to the hairdresser's and to her daughter's home to visit.

But more important than the duties was the attitude with which she cared for Mrs. S. She sat with her, listening to life stories, sharing some of her own. She found Mrs. S. to be attractive and intelligent, a woman who had led an interesting life. At night she placed things on the nightstand so that Mrs. S. could reach them easily. And she said, "I just loved her so much that I hugged her and kissed her good-night "

Living With You

Many times caregivers move parents from their own homes into the caregiver's homes thinking it will ease the care along with the anxiety. This may be a good solution but there are preparations and considerations that should precede the move. As a caregiver, you should ask yourself some important questions before committing yourself to sharing your home with an aging parent and relinquishing your privacy.

Some of those questions are:

What is, and has been, your relationship with the person? If it has been strained or non-communicative in years past, there is no reason to believe that living together will relieve or improve it.

Are there any unforgiven issues that could cause problems of abuse? As I mentioned in an earlier chapter, this was a root problem between my grandmother and me.

What is the temperament of the aged one, and what are the temperaments of those who will be caring for that person? It is important to know the strengths and weaknesses of each in order to understand and relate with each other. For example, if the aged one is a domineering, controlling choleric temperament, and you are also choleric, there will be conflict unless you understand these characteristics and respond with Christ-like love. Knowing the temperaments will help you know what to expect. While you may not be able to change the other person, you can understand and respond with love.

Are the members of your family willing to share their lives, possibly change their lifestyle, to care for this aging person for as long as necessary? The time factor must be considered. No one knows the life span of another, and it could be a week, a month or many years that increasing care will be needed.

Is everyone in your family willing to share the extra household duties as well as the personal care of the aged one?

Is there room in your home for the aged one to live, to have a separate room with personal belongings and to have a private bathroom? When people leave their home, they are torn away from all the familiar things. Many times their contentment will depend on having privacy and personal possessions, as well as a measure of independence within the boundaries of your home.

Have you set guidelines for your time and care? Being a martyr is not going to result in effective care for the person or joy for the caregiver. Caregivers need privacy, time alone with family and spouse, fellowship with friends, shopping time and personal devotion time. This may mean depending on family members to stay with the loved one, or hiring someone to sit in while you take a much-needed break. Since caregivers don't know the length of time for care, these needs should be considered at the outset.

Is your home designed for an additional person? For instance, having the room of your loved one upstairs would require running up and down stairs often, or require the aged one to attempt to negotiate the stairs.

Is your loved one ready to be relegated to a family situation? Loved ones who are still socially active and fairly independent may not adjust to living in a home where schedules must be abided by, or where there are rambunctious children and confusion.

Do you and your spouse have a good relationship? Even the strongest of marriages can be strained when another person enters the home. An extra measure of consideration may be necessary to bolster the relationship.

Do the caregivers have full- or part-time jobs in addition to the responsibility of caregiving? What is the financial situation? Are there health problems in the family that will require additional care, anxiety and finances?

Caring for a loved one in the home means additional burdens, but if the questions are considered and answered honestly, the experience won't be a complete emotional and physical shock.

This honest and heartfelt story was shared with me by a friend, and I've used it here with her permission:

> Ours was a second marriage for both of us, and we hadn't been together many years before my husband's stepfather died. This immediately created a problem as his mother was eighty-two years old and suffering from

osteoporosis. She really couldn't go on living in the mobile home she had shared with her husband, especially since it was in Northern California, twelve hours away from her only child, my husband.

So my husband did the only thing he knew to do. He moved her down to live with us. Now our family included my husband, myself, my two children, and his mother. We did have an extra bedroom for her so there was no disruption there.

People really questioned me regarding how I felt about this move, as some of my friends had already gone through having a parent live with them, and it was rough. I felt I didn't have a choice.

The first year was unbearably hard. Since I had only met his mother on a couple of occasions before she moved in, there was no relationship in our past. We were starting fresh—an old lady who had some very strong ideas of her own and who felt she deserved to live with us, and myself, with my own mother having Alzheimer's disease and going in and out of nursing homes. This made a bad combination right off—I wanted to be able to help my own mother, yet she had to be in a nursing home while I had to do more for another old lady, one I had never even known.

We did not have a family room so the TV and center of the home were in the living room. All day long and until she went to bed at night, my mother-in-law sat (in my favorite rocker) in front of the TV, watching it and controlling it. I worked during the day, so she was home alone. But in the afternoon, when I was tired after a busy day working in our school office and wanted a quiet place to come home to, I walked in to hear the TV blaring. On my days off, the only place I could find for a retreat was my bedroom. I resented having to spend my time there, however, in search of quiet and solitude. I prayed so hard in those days for God to give me a love for this lady who really didn't have anywhere else to go. I struggled to put myself in her place, but all I could think about was that if I were her, I would find a retirement home and live there.

One day I told my husband that this arrangement just wasn't working out. I couldn't stand the stress of having her live with us. He told me that she was staying. If I couldn't take it, I would have to leave. Since it was his house I had moved into, I knew I had no choice. This caused further resentment on my part and we had some stormy months.

Finally, my husband bought his mother her own TV and placed it in her room. This helped the situation. From that time on she stayed in her room most of the time. Even though it was right off the living room and the first room down the hall where she could see everything that was going on, it was a relief to me. Since all she did was watch TV anyway, this was the best solution.

After a while I got more adjusted to her being with us, but it was never easy. We could never go anywhere without having to make ample plans for her, making sure her meals were cooked, etc. Sometimes it was just easier to stay home than to go out somewhere. My children were great, however, and helped as much as possible even though this was not their grandmother. I tried not to let my resentment show and tried to teach them to respect her.

She fell a couple of times and broke some bones, which meant she had some stays in the hospital. As bad as I felt for her, it was a relief for me to have a breather.

Finally, after we buried my own mother and father, my mother-in-law fell and broke her arm. Our doctor said she should not be left alone anymore as she was getting quite confused. The night she fell she couldn't find her way out of the bathroom. She had lived with us five and a half years.

With great remorse and doubt my husband put her in a nursing home. He was very faithful to go by after work and see her every day. She lived at the nursing home until she died at the age of ninety-one.

I now sometimes feel guilty realizing that I felt a certain amount of relief when she went into the nursing home. But I realize that I was put in a very difficult situation. With my own mother suffering and needing care, I was forced to give that care to another person.

If I had felt my husband understood my dilemma I would have done better. But when I had to choose between having her with us or my moving out, it caused me a lot of pain. He said he felt responsible for both of us and this was the only way he knew how to handle the situation. I can understand his concern, but if he had talked to me as an adult and not forced something on me without my consent, I think I would have been able to have her here and feel that I wanted to help.

It was a very hard time in our marriage, but we got through it, and I tried to understand his—and her—feelings. There was no other way. We did try to buy a bigger house, but that didn't work out either. I know that in her better days she was probably a lovely woman, as so many people have told me. I wish I had seen that side of her. It would have been easier on all of us.

This story emphasizes the importance of answering the questions and working together to make the experience acceptable for all concerned.

On the other side, another friend's mother lived with her and it was a happy experience for her whole family. In a questionnaire I sent to her, I asked these questions: How did you know when to begin to care for your loved one? Why did you decide to care for her instead of moving her to a nursing home? How did this affect your life, your family relationships, and your social life? What were some of your greatest emotional struggles? Would you do it again if you had to?

To these questions Cheryl responded:

> When my mother was released from the hospital following major cancer surgery, it was very natural to us to bring her to our home. I never considered a nursing care facility. No one loved my mom as I did so I knew no one could take care of her well enough to please me, nor did I want anyone else to.

> It was a bit of an inconvenience, but loving and living end with dying, so our family accepted it. God gave me a wonderful husband who never questioned our role in all this. He loved my mother and helped a lot.

> Our children learned about love and caring and compassion. My mom took over our bedroom so Cal and I slept in various places, the hide-a-bed in the family room, our queen-size bed set up in the middle of the living room or the bed in the room of our fourteen-year-old son. He was the most displaced. He slept out of his bedroom for about six months.

> The children stayed with Mom a lot at the beginning. They learned to help her out of bed and bring her what she needed. Then it was easy to leave her. If I was the only one going out, my husband cared for her. For special occasions, the nurse stayed more hours or the housekeeper came to stay. I really needed the time away. It made it easier when I came home again. The breaks were important to me and my mom encouraged me too.

> The most difficult time to get help was on Sunday. I needed to be in church every week and many weeks

was unable to do so. Now I see that was minimal but at the time I felt deprived of church attendance.

I think the helplessness was the worst part. There was nothing I could do to make my mom get well. That was extremely hard. Once I accepted the fact that she wasn't going to get well, I tried to spend all the time I could showing her how much she was loved.

Would I do it again? Definitely. I think it lessened my grief when my mother died because I had seen her suffer, and I was relieved to see her released from the pain. Also, I've had nothing to deal with except grief since her death. No guilt.

When asked what she would advise others contemplating home care, Cheryl replied,

Just remember, it's only for a matter of time. It's not going to last forever, and after it's over you will be glad you were there when you were needed.

One evening when I was very tired I sort of lost my temper and cried. My mother said if it were better she would go to a rest home. I didn't want that, I told her, and she didn't either. It was never mentioned again after that.

Taking care of my mom was very painful because I knew it was preparing me to tell her goodbye. The Lord gave me strength I never knew possible. I learned to give her a bath, change her diapers and feed her just like she was one of our children. I never minded doing it and remembered that many years before she had done this for me and my three children whom she adored. I also learned to give her insulin shots and later morphine shots. That also was easy for me to do because I knew I was helping her.

My mom didn't want to die at home but the Lord had other plans. For our family, it was natural for her to die in our home because this was where we had cared for her. We've had no bad effects from this. The same evening she died Charlie was able to go into her room and watch TV just as he had done the night before.

As much as I hated to see her suffer, the Lord gave me a chance to love and care for my mom and get ready to tell her goodbye. If she had died suddenly, I never would have had that privilege.

I talked with many caregivers about bringing their parents in to live with them. Here is another letter, and it expresses honestly the feelings of a woman who cared for her mother-in-law.

I really wanted to take care of her until her death and I'm glad I was able to cope through the entire experience. I don't think I did it out of love and caring, but more out of downright determination to say, "See? All it takes is determination to be able to do what has to be done and what is right."

I resented her for what she did and did not do. I had no respect for her as a woman, a mother or a wife. She was purely self-oriented. However, she was God's child and needed to be treated as such. I think I was guilt-ridden for these thoughts that certainly were not in keeping with God's Word; therefore, I took extra special care of her to compensate ... I'm glad I did what I did and allowed her to remain in her own home for as long as possible and then to move in with her son until her last breath.

As long as our loved ones are healthy, without serious physical and mental problems, and can live independently, the decisions are not particularly pressing. But panic sets in when our loved ones cannot, or should not, live by themselves. Moving them into your home is an option. Now we'll consider the choices of facilities that give care to our aging ones.

Other Options

Shared Homes

There are alternatives to a loved one living either alone or in the home of the caregiver. Many older people are finding that sharing a home with another person can be beneficial to both parties. Perhaps the one sharing the home is another aging person, or a young person in need of housing who is willing to be a helper as well. This means companionship, but also financial relief for both. The costs of rent, utilities and maintenance are shared. Each person has privacy with a room and bath of her (or his) own. According to an article by Genell J. Subak Sharpe and Helene MacLean:

> Home-sharing is a flexible housing option—specific arrangements can be varied according to individual needs—and because the costs of rent and utilities are split between two or more people, it's also economical. In some cases, residents can work out a barter agreement so they provide certain services in the household (such as cleaning or grocery shopping) in lieu of rent.[2]

Home-sharing is an option for aging ones, but it too must be considered with care. When a person has been living alone for many years, or has been used to a spouse's habits, adjusting to a new relationship may take time. Careful evaluation of each person in regard to temperaments, interests, hobbies, pets, allergies, health, habits and food preferences, for example, is a must. The lifestyle similarities and differences should be considered also.

The *AARP New Bulletin*, published by the American Association of Retired Persons, cites the following tips from the National Shared Housing Resource Center:

- Clarify what you want. Are your expectations realistic? If you're looking for a roommate who will cook, clean and pay rent, you'll be disappointed. If you can't let "my" home become "our" home, sharing isn't for you.

- Ask your local office on aging for the name of a home-share program. You can advertise on your own, but it's best to go through friends and relatives or an agency. For your safety, use a post office box for replies.

- Interview potential housemates carefully. Explore differences as well as similarities.

- Set up a trial period. Getting to know one another is the best way to approach home-sharing and make it work.[3]

For more information about home-sharing, including AARP's guide to sharing, write: HO37, AARP, 1909 K Street N.W., Washington, D.C., 20049.

Retirement Complexes

Another option is a retirement home that consists of apartments. Many are built in a quad formation where people watch out for each other, helping those who can't drive to the grocery store or attend church, or who have other needs. My mother and father lived in a retirement apartment in Florida. A neighbor sometimes picked up items at the store for them or took Mom grocery shopping. Even though the church was not far from their apartment, they often were unable to walk that far or my father was unable to push Mom's wheelchair, and the kindly neighbor drove them to the church.

At the same complex there was a nursing facility for those who could no longer live by themselves and needed nursing care.

Many retirement complexes today are planned to meet the special needs of aging people. Subak-Sharpe and Mac-Lean report that there are many options available:

The possibilities are much broader and include rental apartments, co-ops, condominiums, one-family cottages and the increasingly popular "life-care" communities, where services keep pace with the changing needs of the residents. Amenities range from simple housekeeping help to home-health care and to 24-hour nursing care, when necessary.[4]

Extended Homes

Another option for care of aging parents is an apartment within the home such as I mentioned earlier in the book. When Shirley's mother could no longer live alone and care for her own needs, the decision was made to sell her mobile home and build a bedroom/bath/living-room addition onto Shirley's home. This arrangement gave her mother a place with her own possessions, the security of a family, no responsibility for cooking meals and a safe place to live.

Along this same idea is the studio-type cottage or a mobile home on the same property. This gives the loved one a place of his or her own close enough to receive help when needed without interfering with the family structure in the home.

Board-and-Care Homes

Board-and-care homes are an option if loved ones do not require nursing care. These homes rent rooms where the aging ones can have their own belongings, according to the regulations of the home, and the meals are supplied. Communal dining and living rooms are available that give a home-like atmosphere.

My grandmother was in good health, although unable to live alone, when we found a board-and-care home near us. She had a nice large room and well-cooked meals. Her linen was changed and washed periodically. She shared a bathroom with other residents. I visited her regularly, and took her shopping and to church. This gave her respite from the home and the security of family nearby.

Nanny was well cared for until she became ill and the staff could not provide the nursing care she required. It was then that we moved her to our home.

Just as with any care facility, the board-and-care home should be checked out. Find out if it is licensed and has met health standards as set by the local Board of Health. A first-hand visit to inspect the home will tell whether the home is clean and well heated and has met safety standards for elderly people. By talking with residents, you can tell whether they are cheerful and content or morose and depressed. Is there any sign of abuse among the residents? Are the kitchen facilities clean and is the food fresh and well prepared? Talk with families of those who have had loved ones at the particular home.

When all the options are considered, and all conditions point to the need for continual skilled nursing care, a nursing home may be your only choice.

Nursing Homes

When it became necessary to move my mother and father into a nursing home, we didn't like the idea. Nursing homes to us were places for the very old and infirm. Our folks weren't old to us—they simply were in need of care that we couldn't provide. To our dismay, the attitude of the staff toward my mother was not acceptable. It bordered on abuse by neglect, not affording her the dignity she deserved during the last stage of her life.

It was when my sister confronted the head nurse about her attitude, and when my sister, brother and I showed love and concern for Mom as she lay dying, that the attitude of the staff changed. When we cared and loved, they began to care. Mom's death had an impact that we will never forget. The nurses' aides came to the funeral, bringing long-stemmed roses in a glass vase and a large card they had made that said, "Love made the sky open up and God smiled through." Perhaps this is the key to care for our loved ones. When a loved one is visited and shown consideration and respect, nurses and staff will reflect that same respectful attitude.

A short article in *Modern Maturity* magazine titled, "Nursing Homes Need Kindly Hands," reported a study in abuse of aged patients by University of New Hampshire researchers Karl Pillemer, Ph.D., and David Moore, Ph.D. Their survey of 577 staff members from 57 nursing homes showed:

> Thirty-six percent reported seeing at least one incident of physically abusive behavior in the past year, with excessive... restraint of patients the most frequent type; this was followed by pushing, grabbing, shoving and pinching. Fully 81 percent observed at least one instance of psychological abuse: Yelling or swearing at a patient in anger was cited as most common... 10 percent of the respondents admitted having themselves committed an act of physical abuse; 40 percent, one of psychological abuse.[5]

Pillemer blamed this condition on the fact that the employees are "often poorly trained in the interpersonal aspects of care and placed in extremely stressful situations."[6]

Don McLeod in an article, "Abuse Abounds," substantiates the findings of Pillemer and Moore. A survey of health care professionals conducted by the Department of Health and Human Services found that "nearly all the respondents indicate abuse is a problem in nursing homes... Most of the perceived abuse was attributed to overworked and undertrained aides and orderlies."[7]

The article concludes, "The number one form of abuse reported was neglect, both physical and emotional."[8]

As the number of elderly increases, society has become more aware of the problems of care. Nursing home standards and the quality of care have come out of the darkness, revealing abuses and poor treatment. The government, and others who are concerned about their aging loved ones, have initiated programs for change and for holding nursing staffs accountable for their actions.

State-by-state guides to 15,000 quality care nursing homes have been prepared and are available from the U.S. Government Printing Office in Washington, D.C. These guides report on nursing homes that have or have not met quality care standards set by the Bureau of Health Standards and Quality. The standards cover Medicaid and Medicare requirements, patient care and abuse, and the home itself.[9]

Although there are negative aspects to nursing homes, and conditions are stressful with undertrained and underpaid staff, this is not always the case. Many nursing homes have caring people on their staff.

My daughter, Lori, worked in a nursing home when she was sixteen. She had two weeks of training that consisted of learning practical care of the elderly: how to bathe, feed and dress those who were unable to care for themselves; how to lift them in bed, helping them from bed to chair and back; how to place a bedpan with the least discomfort and most efficiency.

Another important aspect of the training was learning to make a bed properly. While this seems like a small thing, aged people who lie in bed most of the time have thin and sensitive skin that chafes and blisters easily. A wrinkled sheet is uncomfortable and can cause sores.

The training also touched on the emotional needs of the aged ones.

Most important for Lori, she liked the people she served. She talked with them while helping them, listening as they shared with her. In the evening she prayed with and for them. She told me, "Praying with them was a special time for them. I felt they probably were there to die, but my being able to share Jesus gave them hope for living and hope for dying as well."

Lori continued, "There was a particular woman who was real grouchy. I remember praying for her as I got her ready for bed. I realized that I needed to see her as a person in a difficult situation, rather than reacting to her outward appearance of grouchiness."

Lori related several stories about people she remembered from her nursing home days, saying, "I became quite attached to these people, and continued to correspond with them long after I stopped working there."

She told the story of Lynn (not her real name), a thirty-five-year-old woman who was stricken with multiple sclerosis. Her husband had left her, and when she felt she could no longer care for her little girl, she gave her up for adoption. Lynn was a lonesome, heartbroken woman, disillusioned by life and her religion.

Lori began to listen to Lynn as she cared for her and talked with her about Jesus. She prayed with and for Lynn, and one day led her to salvation through Jesus Christ. Lynn's attitude changed as she began to see herself as God's child. Lori gave her a Bible and loaned her books by Corrie ten Boom, Eugenia Price and others so that she could read and grow in her faith.

A pastor and his wife from a neighboring town took Lynn beyond the walls of the nursing home to their own home. There she baked cookies and enjoyed being involved in a home situation. They took her to church to give her spiritual uplifting too.

Although Lynn was not elderly, she was in the same predicament as our aged ones, needing the same physical, emotional and spiritual care.

Long after Lori stopped working at the nursing home she corresponded with Lynn and visited whenever she could.

Charlie was another elderly patient whom Lori loved and talked with. She discovered he had always harbored the dream of going to Alaska. After Lori's return from her Alaskan trip, she visited Charlie and took her pictures to share with him.

As a caregiver, Lori tried to relate with the people, realizing they were in difficult circumstances. Although these people may be shells of their former selves, there is still that spark of life yet to be lived, and a lifetime of experience to be shared.

If you are thinking of a nursing home for your aged one, the attitude of the caregivers is as important to consider as the physical facilities.

When caregivers, whether professional in a nursing home or family members in private care, look beyond the outward age and condition to the life that is still in that aged one, they see that person from another perspective—God's perspective. Conditions may be stressful and pay may be inadequate, but what the caregivers focus on will determine to a great extent what their attitude toward the aged ones will be.

There are those who make the jobs of the nursing home staff easier. These are people who love the elderly and volunteer to sit with them, read to them, feed them or take them out for walks or rides. A friend of mine makes this a ministry as she visits a nursing home. I was with her as she readied one elderly person for a "walk" in her wheelchair. What appreciation I saw as that aged woman commented on the colorful flowers, a new building, the people on the street and the children passing by. Nothing escaped her notice.

Another friend, Donna, is a retired nurse who conducts a weekly Bible study in a nursing home. When she goes in, the people are slumped in their chairs, yet when they see her their eyes light up. She brings them hope, and they recognize that she cares for them.

Donna thought one elderly man couldn't talk, but when she returned after several weeks' absence he said, "I didn't know if you were coming again."

How do you find the right nursing home? Begin by visiting the various homes, keeping your senses alert to what kind of home it is. What do your senses tell you? Are the grounds well-kept with flowers and smooth, well-constructed walkways? Are the windows clean? Are the floors vacuumed and shiny?

At Christmas a group of us went caroling at a nursing home. When we stepped inside the door, we were impressed with the comfortable and pretty furniture. The chairs were covered with what looked like a lovely flowered chintz material, but it was plastic—easy to clean yet comfortable to sit on. The colors were soft, restful mauves and greens. The floors shone and evidence everywhere indicated that the place was well kept.

The patients were at dinner when we sang to them. They wore pretty sweaters, and their white hair was neatly combed and clean. There was no repugnant odor about those aged ones as we went from one to another wishing them a Merry Christmas. They responded cheerfully to our singing and our personal greetings.

The staff members were neat and friendly. They welcomed us and seemed genuinely happy to have us there. One of them sat with an elderly lady, gently rubbing her back and neck as she ate her light supper. We observed while we sang that the attitude seemed to be one of caring.

The food looked appropriate and was fresh and served attractively.

What I saw, heard, smelled and touched gave me the impression that I would not object to my parents living in that home. If I were to go further, I would inspect the rooms and see if the patients had their personal belongings, and if the staff respected those belongings. I would check on safety features in individual bedrooms and bathrooms.

I would inspect the kitchen facilities and taste the food, observing how it was stored and prepared. I would note the appearance of the cooks, their physical appearance and cleanliness as well as their working clothes, and how well they cared for their kitchen. I like clean, shiny and uncluttered counters and well-organized cupboards, clean dishes and silverware to eat from, and clean pots to cook in.

I would also talk with those who live there to hear the perspective from the inside. Many times the elderly don't talk much but they see and hear what is going on around them, and everything is making its impression.

Nursing home employees who are proud of their facilities will not object to such an inspection. Rather, they will invite and welcome people who care enough to want to know. I would be wary of a nursing home where the odor is strong and disagreeable, or where the residents are sitting in chairs lined up in the halls, slumped and in disarray showing disrespect toward their personhood, or where the staff appears slovenly and uncaring or careless in their appearance or conversation.

A good rule of thumb would be to imagine yourself in that home if you were old and infirm. Would it be a place and a staff you would be willing to entrust yourself to?

In considering all the options for your loved ones, the choices will depend on each particular situation. The decision that falls to the caregiver must be made objectively and practically, as well as subjectively. Consider your loved ones' emotional, physical and financial conditions, consider your situation carefully and try not to wait until the time is upon you to make the decision.

Preparation is one of the best ways of dealing with the care of your aging loved one. Age doesn't happen instantaneously and, although it is difficult to think of your parents needing drastic care, the future must be faced with practicality and loving concern.

———

Evaluating the housing needs of your aging loved ones is an important part in the caregiving process. When you are faced with this decision, consider the options for them:

- Live at home with safety modifications and basic help.
- Live at home with a live-in caregiver.
- Live at home using city, county or private home health care.

- Share their home with a young person or another older person.

- Live in a board-and-care home with no skilled nursing care.

- Live in an extended home within your home: apartment, mobile home or separate cottage.

- Live in a separate room within your home with cooperation of the entire family.

- Move to a nursing home after careful inspection of the facility. Remember that a loving and caring attitude on your part will influence the care and respect your aged one receives from others.

9

Knowing the Finances

The decisions concerning long-term care of your aging loved ones must be made carefully and prayerfully, considering both the loved ones and the caregiver. One of the main issues to confront is the harsh reality of finances.

In deciding whether your loved ones should live independently in their own home or be moved to a care facility, the financial condition must be discussed. To move aging ones too soon might deplete assets before the intensive care begins. It is wise to evaluate their condition and use every resource you can to help them, so that when and if the time comes for constant care, the assets will be available.

As care moves from stage to stage, the costs will probably multiply. Making safety changes in their home, hiring part- or full-time help, or using community services may be more taxing on the caregiver, but it will allow your loved ones to live within their own means for a longer period of time. The length of time that any kind of care will be needed is unpredictable, and that means prudence must be exercised in the handling of assets.

Controlling Assets

Many aging ones refuse to discuss their financial situation with an "outsider" even if that person is their own child.

111

Divulging personal financial information exposes an intimate part of one's self, so it is not unusual for aging loved ones to jealously guard knowledge of their assets. As physical strength diminishes with age, so also does the security of taking care of themselves diminish. Their money becomes their security and if they lose control of that, they feel helpless.

As my father aged and became incapacitated by his stroke, he became more and more money-conscious. He wanted to know how much they had in their checking and savings accounts at all times. He worried about spending money and about the cost of things.

When caregivers approach the subject of finances, they must realize the formidable circumstances of age. Old age should be prepared for just as parents plan for college expenses for their children, except that there are no scholarships for old age care. Assets of the elderly are to be used for their care until they die or until the money runs out. There are those who feel that money intended as inheritance is squandered when funding care. However, what the aged have reaped through their lives belongs to them as long as they live.

Wills

Many aging parents refuse to make wills or even discuss the subject. A will means death and people don't like to face the fact that someday they will cease to exist. But to avoid the issue is to deny the inevitable.

My father-in-law was a strong and independent man who had supported his family well through the years. However, when his health failed and it became necessary for his daughter to care for him, he stubbornly refused to discuss a will. It was only when he realized his assets would be distributed according to the laws of the state and his heirs would be the losers that he consented to it.

Every adult should have a will even if the assets are small and seem insignificant. What happens to the house, car, personal belongings, final paycheck, savings and even underage children will be decided by the courts and may not be according to the person's desires. Not having a will causes problems for loved ones—problems that with a little planning can be avoided.

Various kinds of wills can be drawn up, but the process need not be complicated. A simple will, leaving assets to a surviving spouse or to surviving heirs, is uncomplicated and expresses your wishes in the disbursement of assets.

If your parents are reluctant to discuss a will, one approach is to appeal to their desire to decide who benefits from their years of toil and saving. If you as the caregiver haven't made a will, this may be the appropriate time to invite an attorney to a meeting with you and your parents to explain the needs and advantages of various documents and discuss what is appropriate for each of you.

Living Trusts

Many people are becoming aware of the cost and length of time involved in probate and are placing their assets in a living trust. This method avoids probate and names a beneficiary who immediately becomes the administrator of the trust (assets) upon the death of the trustee.

After the death of my first husband and the sale of my house, a financial consultant advised me to place my invested funds in a living trust. The income from the investments is mine to use as I choose for my lifetime. Upon my death the beneficiary will administer the funds according to my will.

When I remarried, the terms of my living trust remained the same, and my heirs will still receive the inheritance from that trust. A simple will bequeaths my joint assets and my share of my husband's assets to him if he survives me.

Power of Attorney

Another weighty issue is power of attorney. This assigns to one person the power to act on behalf of another—to sign checks and make financial decisions. However, it is for a limited time and is rendered invalid when the loved one becomes incapacitated.

A power of attorney may be the solution in the case of one who becomes ill, has surgery, or for some other reason is unable to pay bills and make appropriate decisions. When the person is restored and once again physically and mentally capable of making decisions and handling affairs, the power of attorney is no longer needed. Power of attorney does not give the person the right to make major legal, medical or life-affecting decisions should the loved one become incompetent. This can only be done with a *durable power of attorney*, which is made when the loved one is in good mental health and aware of the contents of the document. A durable power of attorney safeguards the aged one from decisions made by physicians, the courts or others who would not be directly concerned with his care.

Protection and Arrangements

According to a booklet from AARP, *Domestic Mistreatment of the Elderly—Towards Prevention*, taking measures that anticipate future care can reduce the likelihood of neglect or abuse.[1]

When aging ones take steps to protect themselves, the one chosen as their representative must be a person of integrity who is willing to accept the responsibility for necessary decisions and who has love and concern for the best interest of the aged ones.

If an elderly person has not assigned his or her care to a particular person and becomes incapacitated, the court has the right to appoint a guardian. The guardian may or may not consider the best interest of the aged one, and decisions may be made over which relatives or other interested persons have no control.

At the time I was caring for my parents I was unaware of these measures, but the method we chose was right for us because my parents were mentally competent. They agreed to place my name on their savings and checking accounts, with survivorship rights. I was able to withdraw funds at their request to pay airfare when I took them to Florida for the winter, or for emergencies, as when my mother had congestive heart failure. I had the ability to pay bills when my mother was no longer able to manage her affairs, and to pay funeral costs at the end. Since the accounts were legally mine after their deaths, I was responsible to divide that money according to their wishes expressed in the will.

Funeral arrangements also can be made before loved ones die. Many aging ones buy burial lots and express their funeral wishes to those close to them. I was with my mother and father when they chose their burial lots overlooking the river. It was important to them to have this matter settled, and it certainly lessened the stress during our time of grief.

I remember the day my mother expressed her wish for her funeral service. Her desire was that her casket be laid in her familiar place, in front of the sunny bay windows of the farm, rather than the community church or funeral home.

Mortuaries have prepaid plans where expenses are taken care of before death. However, these must be considered carefully. You should compare several plans as to price, what is included, and any hidden expenses. For information on prepaid funerals, write to:

"Product Report: Prepaying Your Funeral?" (D13188)
AARP Fulfillment (EE064)
1909 K Street N.W.
Washington, D.C. 20049

Other information that will help in the final stages of caregiving includes knowing where the will is located, how much insurance is available and the company that holds the policy, savings and checking account numbers, safe combination or location of the key, and the location and number of the safe deposit box. Placing the caregiver's name on the safe deposit box allows access to the will, deeds or other important documents without a waiting period.

Every person has handled the affairs of life uniquely. Make a checklist of what concerns you and your loved ones, and work with them as much as possible in simplifying your life and theirs. Talk with an attorney to gain an understanding of the various documents and the particular needs of your loved ones.

The way caregivers approach these delicate matters will make a difference in the willingness of the loved ones to cooperate. Understanding the emotions of the aged, their feelings of helplessness, loss of autonomy, dislike of dependency and admission of the finality of life will help caregivers have more patient and loving attitudes.

It is wise to have family councils during caregiving years to avoid misunderstandings and bitterness in the final accounting. Meeting with family members to discuss care, financial arrangements and responsibilities, assets and plans can also be healthy for future relationships after the loved ones are gone.

One family I know of still has bitter feelings because of undiscussed and unresolved difficulties after their father died. Several family members acted without consent of the others and buried their dad in a distant place instead of in the family plot beside his wife. After the funeral, more hard feelings were created by a lack of sensitivity and respect in dividing personal belongings. These bitter feelings might never have arisen if the family members had talked together earlier and discussed issues out of love for each other and their father.

Medicare and Medicaid help for long-term care is changing with various legislation. Many bills are before the House of Representatives and Senate to change long-term care funding. Write your congressman to learn what is happening. Legislators are realizing that with the increasing years of care, more efficient funding is necessary. Being aware of Medicare and Medicaid coverage and changes can help avoid confusion about who is eligible and what is covered or not covered by the plans.

Learning to fill out medical forms and keeping accurate records are necessary when approaching insurance companies or Medicare for payment. A record book of doctor visits, medications and other medical facts eliminates guesswork and confusion.

The financial dilemma for long-term care can be frightening. You must plan carefully, use assets and resources wisely, and prayerfully handle long-term care one day at a time.

———

Perhaps the most sensitive issue you'll have to talk about as a family is the area of finances. When you are faced with the financial situation of caregiving:

- Take stock of all assets and resources.
- Plan carefully for future care.
- Don't panic or move too quickly.
- Approach your aging ones with love and prayer:
  - To make a will
  - To grant power of attorney/durable power of attorney
  - To help you keep records by sharing information about insurance policies, safe deposit boxes, deeds, bank accounts, and so on
  - To place assets in a living trust if appropriate
- Become knowledgeable about Medicare programs and legislation concerning long-term care.

- Keep accurate records.
- Talk with an attorney about needs and appropriate steps to take.
- Keep the family apprised of the financial situation.

10

Knowing Your Resources

W here do I go and to whom do I turn for help? Caregivers often ask these questions when they find they cannot do everything on their own. Due to extended longevity and ever-increasing care needs, more resources for the caregiver have arisen to help with the challenge.

While each situation is unique, there are those who can help if we know the resources available to us—but it isn't enough just to know what is available. We also need to call upon those who are ready and willing to come to our aid. According to an article in *Psychology Today*, "Family caregivers generally make scant use of community services such as adult day-care centers and respite care."[1]

My parents lived in a small town where organized services for the elderly were not available. The services in my town, even meals-on-wheels, were twenty miles away. But when I cared for my mother and father, I neglected to call upon those in the community who loved my folks and would have gladly given their help.

Cheryl, who cared for her mother in her home, hired a visiting nurse after her mom's stroke. The nurse came to her home two or three times a week to check vital signs and answer questions. This service was helpful, but not as much as the friend she hired for the housekeeping who also bathed her mom. This gave Cheryl a much-needed break.

Her mother's insurance paid for a nurse in the home as many hours as needed. Cheryl said, "We started with eight hours a day from 2 P.M. to 10 P.M. so I could be free to cook dinner for my family uninterrupted. It worked very well. At the end we were having ten- to twelve-hour shifts and I was the night caregiver."

One caregiver who cared for her mother for eleven years after the death of her father hired a woman to spend four hours a day with her mother while she was at work. The woman fixed lunch and sometimes dinner. This arrangement worked until illness forced her to place her mother in a nursing home.

During her caregiving years, my sister took advantage of various resources. She sought social services for help in nursing-home placement and found the visiting nurses were "great when you needed them," but the home health personnel not as helpful for her particular needs.

Many times our best resources are close by. Each caregiver's needs differ and each area offers different benefits. Therefore, you must be creative in discovering and making the most of available resources.

Creative caregiving is when the caregiver assesses the community resources, then follows through with a request for assistance. The following are suggestions for help in your caregiving responsibilities:

Call upon family members and friends. This might be to bring in a meal or sit with your aging one. It could be as simple as picking up the mail from the mailbox and taking it to the house.

One of my fears was that my father would fall going to the mailbox. But rather than call upon a neighbor or request that the mail be delivered directly to their door, I foolishly braved icy roads from my house to take the mail in for them. Many times people wait to be asked and are more than willing to accommodate the caregiver, but they don't want to interfere if their help is not solicited.

Call local high schools or colleges to find young people who are fond of the elderly and need part-time work. Young people often relate well with the elderly and will do an excellent job caring for them. Church youth groups seeking a ministry of service are willing to do a variety of jobs that are needed as well.

Widows and widowers or older people who are lonely or wanting to feel useful may find sitting and chatting with an aged person mutually beneficial. If the aged one is able, a trip to the mall just to watch the activity, or out to lunch or to attend church functions may give him (or her) a much enjoyed outing, benefit the helper through companionship, and relieve the caregiver all at the same time.

Many churches and communities have established support groups for caregivers. Members of these groups help and encourage each other in the care of themselves as well as their aging loved ones. For those who are seeking a support group, Children of Aging Parents (CAP) has a publication list that can be obtained by sending a self-addressed envelope to:

CAP
2761 Trenton Rd.
Levittown, PA 19056

Some churches have initiated programs for the elderly such as adult day-care centers. Caregivers can leave their loved ones in the morning and pick them up in the evening. For those seeking adult day-care centers in their area, a directory listing 847 centers in 46 states can be obtained by writing to the National Council on Aging:

NCOA Publications
P.O. Box 7227
Ben Franklin Station
Washington, DC 20044

Organizations

The main objective of the **Gray Panthers** organization is to serve as an advocate for the elderly, according to Rachel Zane of the Tucson chapter. The Panthers keep abreast of all legislative and medical issues pertaining to the elderly and of developments in financial aid programs. While they are not service-oriented, they work in conjunction with other agencies.

Rachel was enthusiastic about their Project Match. This is a program where individuals who are in reasonably good health, but who either can't afford to support a home or are lonely and desire companionship, are matched with another person with similar interests, intelligence and desires.

Other housing options designed by the Gray Panthers are Congregate Housing and Surrogate Housing. Both of these programs serve much-needed housing demands of the elderly.

The Gray Panthers organization is valuable, not only for the elderly but also for the caregiver. It is a dynamic, forward-looking organization with projects designed to meet future needs and to improve programs already in force. Contact the Gray Panthers at their national office in Philadelphia, (215) 545-6555, for more information on groups in your area.

Alzheimer's Association International helps families of Alzheimer's disease victims, conducts research and helps educate the public about Alzheimer's. If you need help with a loved one who has become a victim of this disease, call (800) 621-0379 to locate a chapter in your area.

Alzheimer's Disease and Related Disorders Association of San Diego, Inc. offers support to families of those suffering with Alzheimer's, stroke, Parkinson's disease, or other brain disorders. For information and referral, call (619) 295-2509.

The Southern Regional Resource Center in San Diego, California, is a program of Sharp Memorial Hospital for adults with brain impairment and their caregivers. For information, call (619) 541-4432 or write to:

SRRC
3665 Ruffin Rd., Suite 110
San Diego, CA 92123

Community Resources

Hospitals in your area may have programs especially for elderly care such as adult day-care, a respite program with overnight care, home health care services, and a hospice program where volunteers serve in many different ways both in the home and in facilities.

Ombudsmen serve as advocates of the aging. These helpers have been called "gentle warriors."[2] Ombudsmen are mediators for the rights of the aged. When complaints are made by an aged person or by others who suspect violations or abuse, the ombudsman will investigate and follow up on the problem. For information about ombudsmen, call your local area agency on aging, or the state area agency on aging or human services department. You can write for a state-by-state list of long-term ombudsman offices by requesting the AARP publication, "Nursing Home Life: A Guide for Residents and Family" at:

AARP Fulfillment
P.O. Box 22738
Long Beach, CA 90801

The local telephone directory is a valuable resource, helping caregivers locate many community and government organizations. In the Yellow Pages you may find:

Area Agency on Aging
Senior Citizens' Service Organizations
Senior Citizens' Services
Medical Support Groups
Meals-on-Wheels
American Red Cross

American Heart Association
Home Health Services
Mediation Services
Criminal Justice Services
Dispute Resolution Centers

A Legal Rights Calendar gives answers to legal issues affecting older persons. For more information, please contact:

Legal Rights Calendar
P.O. Box 96474
Washington, DC 20049

Publications

A list of state agencies is available from:

National Association of State Units on Aging
2033 K Street NW Suite 304
Washington, DC 20006

The following booklets are available from the American Association for Retired Persons (AARP):

Caregiving
A Handbook About Care in the Home: Information on Home
    Health Services (D955)
Coping and Caring: Living With Alzheimer's Disease
    (D12441)
Miles Away and Still Caring: A Guide for Long Distance
    Caregivers (D12748)

Being Alone
AARP Guide for Widowed Persons: A Checklist of
    Concerns/Resources (D12895)
A Path for Caregivers (D12957)

Home or Alternate Care Facilities
Nursing Home Life: A Guide for Residents and Families

The Doable Renewable Home: Making Your Home Fit Your
Needs (D12143)
A Home Away From Home: Consumer Information on Board-
and-Care Homes (D12446)
The Right Place at the Right Time: A Guide to Long-Term
Care Choices (D12381)
Making Wise Decisions on Long-Term Care (D12435)

Health Care
More Health for Your Dollar: An Older Person's Guide to
Health Maintenance Organizations (HMO) (D1195)
Choosing An HMO: An Evaluation Checklist (D12444)
Healthy Questions: How to Talk to and Select Physicians,
Dentists, and Vision Care Specialists (D12094)

Insurance and Finances
Insurance Checklist (D1032)
Before You Buy: A Guide to Long-Term Care Insurance
(D12893)
Prepaying Your Funeral: Some Questions to Ask (D12639)
Final Details: A State-Specific Guide for Survivors When
Death Occurs (please indicate which state)

These booklets are well written and informative. AARP is
alert to the needs of the aged. The *AARP News Bulletin* keeps
pace with legislation on long-term care funding, what is
happening in Medicare and other medical programs, and
social security developments. It also offers articles of interest to the elderly as well as to the caregiver. For more
information, please write:

AARP Fulfillment
1909 K Street, N.W.
Washington, DC 20049

Funeral Information
Public Reference
Federal Trade Commission
7th & Penn. Ave. N.W., Room 130
Washington, DC 20580

List of Government Publications on Aging
United States Government Printing Office
Superintendent of Documents
Washington, DC 20402

Medicare
"Guide to Health Insurance for People with Medicare"
Consumer Information Center
P.O. Box 100
Pueblo, CO 81002

"Supplemental Medicare Premium"
IRS Publication #934

Knowing Your Rights (available from AARP: D12330)

Legal Information
A recent development in the legal field is the specialization
of attorneys in eldercare. They are knowledgeable about all
areas that concern the elderly. For a free brochure regarding
these Elder Law Attorneys, write:

National Academy of Elder Law Attorneys, Inc.
Dept. MM, 655 N. Alvernon Way, Suite 108
Tucson, AZ 85711

The responsibility of caring for our aging loved ones has
become a concern for our communities, our government and
our churches. Families and caregivers can take heart that
there is help available. As the awareness grows, even more
help will become available. Caregivers who plan carefully

and become familiar with these resources will find that responsibility shared is a lightened load.

Our most valuable resource is One whom we may overlook in the panic and exhaustion of caregiving responsibilities. God is our best resource: "It is He who has made us, and not we ourselves" (Psalm 100:3). He knows us by name and He understands the trials we go through. He knows our loved ones—and the duration of their lives. He will guide us to further resources, enabling us to accomplish the task He has set before us. With His strength we will be enabled to do what we must, and we will reap His blessings for a job well done.

———

It is important to remember as a caregiver that you're not alone. There are resources available and a number of people and places to turn to for help:

- Family and friends
- Local resource groups, high schools, colleges, church youth groups
- Church programs and support groups
- Hospital services, adult day-care centers, respite and hospice care
- Community programs and organizations
- Government services
- Organizations such as Gray Panthers and AARP
- Mediation with ombudsmen
- God—He is your best resource

PART III

The Focus

11

Refocusing on Personal Needs

The years before my folks went to Florida for the winter were extremely difficult for me. The twenty-mile drive to their home, often on icy roads, was a chore. Why didn't I call upon people in the town where we had lived for a lifetime?

My mother and father were not invalids, yet I felt I had to go to them every day, to make beds and clean the bathroom, do the dishes and get their meals so Mom wouldn't have to. I could have called upon neighbors to bring in the mail or a meal, but I didn't want to impose on anyone. Besides, I carried an air of martyrdom—of doing it all myself because I was indispensable. Perhaps I was trying somehow to compensate for my parents' losses and ease my guilt feelings for being young and strong.

I was wrong not to consider my options and the resources available to me. For the icy driveway I could have called someone to plow and sand. Kind people were willing but were never asked to fix a lunch or dinner, or just to step in and see that everything was in order.

My sister lived in the same town and was busy with the foster home she and her husband operated, but I could have asked her teenage son to help. He would have willingly brought dinner from their kitchen to the grandparents he loved. This would have brought joy to my folks to have a visit from their grandson, along with a well-cooked meal. We deprive others of the blessing of being needed, of giving of themselves, when we exclude them.

Sometimes we feel abandoned by our families when we are faced with insurmountable responsibilities. We need to set aside our pride and our guilt feelings and ask for help. Even if there is little organized assistance for your aging parents in your area, there are usually those who would step in to give you some relief.

When Nanny lived with us I felt trapped, yet I don't remember asking my children to stay with her so I could go out to shop or relax for a while. They would have done that gladly if we had planned our caregiving better. The mother of one of our teenager's friends offered to come and sit with Nanny several times and I took advantage of her offers. My husband, too, benefited by sending me off to Maine with our children because I came back spiritually and emotionally refreshed. In many instances it was my own attitude that worked against me.

Caregivers need to delegate some responsibilities so the entire weight of the burden doesn't fall on one person. Responsibilities that could be shared include doing the laundry, making a meal once a week, changing bed linens or tidying the house. While this won't eliminate the day-to-day pressure and exhaustion, it will give a much-needed breather to the caregiver. If you work outside your home, a budget should include help with housecleaning or other chores on a regular basis.

Taking Time for Yourself

Those who take on the duties of caregiving often feel they have given up the right to any sort of refreshment or renewal for themselves. It seems to be an all-or-nothing situation. They tend to pour every bit of energy into caring. What caregivers fail to realize is that they will be more effective in their care and more loving in their attitude if they occasionally are able to "regroup" mentally, physically and spiritually. Some of the best activities for refreshment and renewal are simple and don't require a great deal of time or money, such as going to the beauty parlor to have your hair done, or having a manicure, or the wonderful luxury of a pedicure. Just to be pampered and let someone else be the "caregiver" for a little while can make you feel renewed. If you want to go a little further in relaxation, have a facial and body massage.

Another way to relax is to go shopping even if you don't need anything. Try on pretty and extravagant clothes just for fun. Take a friend with you and try on hats, have a cup of tea or, better still, cappuccino in a cafe. Talk and laugh. Laughter is like jogging and revives the body as well as the soul.

The night before my mother died, we stood around her bed with the pastor, talking and laughing. I don't remember what we were laughing about but it lightened the sorrow we were to face. I believe that Mom, if she could have heard us, would have been pleased because she loved laughter.

In the days following my first husband's death, my children and I laughed at small, silly things. A friend encouraged us, and she also reminded us that people might not understand our laughter. We felt it was a gift from the Lord to help us with the heaviness of grief.

One of my favorite places to go when I feel a need to get away is the library. It has all the latest magazines, the chairs are comfortable—and it is quiet. You can read, or write, or just lean back and close your eyes and think. It is a friendly place where you won't be disturbed.

You can walk in the woods, or on the beach, or in the park—and find a place where you can sit in the sun and feel the breeze on your face. It doesn't take a long time; even a short interlude is an effective antidote to weariness of mind and body. It is a time to think—not negative thoughts but pleasant things, the loveliness and beauty of God. You can allow your mind to roam free and let Him fill it with His thoughts.

Take a soothing bubble bath to soak tired muscles while a tape of your favorite music plays. Times like these will enable you to go on. Anticipate and plan for these escapes as much as any vacation, and they will continuously sustain you.

Use time spaces each day to lift your eyes to the Lord for grace and strength to meet the obligations before you. You may not have time for a prolonged devotional, but brief moments of meditation will renew your mind and refill your spirit.

Time spaces come when you are doing things like driving, vacuuming, ironing or cooking, and your hands are busy but your mind is free. These are times to bring your thoughts into oneness with God's thoughts—thinking on those things that are true, honorable, right, pure, lovely, of good repute, according to Philippians 4:8. Paul goes on to say, "If there is *any* excellence and if *anything* worthy of praise, let your mind dwell on these things" (NASB, italics mine).

We have to take responsibility for what goes into our minds. Many times our minds revolve around the problems, hurts, verbal abuse or other emotional pain, and there is no relaxation, no renewal and no solutions. We must look for anything at all that is positive in the situation and think about that rather than the negatives.

The drive from my folks' home to mine was a time to pray, to come before God with my blunders, tiredness and frustrations. It was a time to memorize Scripture and meditate. I didn't always take advantage of that time space, but it did serve as a transition from caregiver to homemaker, wife and mother.

Make Active Use of Your Time

Slouching in front of the television might feel like the only activity you have energy for, but unfortunately little of television fare is encouraging, edifying or energizing. The exertion of exercise may not appeal to a tired body, but disciplining yourself to take a short walk or bike ride will stimulate you, make you feel alive, enhance your appetite and help you sleep more restfully.

While I lived in Hawaii, I worked in a tennis shop. The job was not physically tiring, yet I went home weary with the desire to lie down for a nap. From my window one evening I saw two ladies jogging, and convinced myself that a lively run would be good for me. With reluctance I put on my shoes and went for a two-mile run. During the run I observed the storms over the mountains, the sound of the surf against the distant cliffs and the beauty around me. The mental and physical exhilaration dissipated my weariness and I was able to eat a healthy supper and have a productive evening.

Many times caregivers don't take time to eat properly. Along with exercise, good nutrition is a key factor in your well-being. Eating slowly while enjoying good conversation or music will help your digestion and renew your energy.

Take time for yourself, to quiet your heart and mind, without guilt. There is no accusation with God. "The joy of the Lord is your strength," says Nehemiah. This joy comes from the inner assurance that God is in control of your situation and that He will bring it to its proper conclusion.

Take time for a personal and intimate relationship with the Lord. He is your helper, your enabler, your friend, the One who will never leave you nor forsake you. To be too busy for the Lord is to deprive ourselves of peace of heart and mind and strength to go on. If you are married, take time for your husband or wife. Walk together, or share a quiet cup of coffee, or spend an evening away from it all. Many times the guilt settles in like thick fog and we can see no further than our circumstances. We feel we can't take time for romantic or companionable intervals. But if we do take the time, and arrange for someone to fill in for us, we are doing good to both ourselves and our loved ones.

Guilt can keep you and your loved ones from utilizing helpful resources. Yet these have been established to benefit those who are in your situation, to make caregiving less lonely by sharing the load. It is your responsibility to use them.

One of these resources is a support group for those going through the same problems, suffering the same frustrations, exhaustion and emotional stress. Talking releases the tensions and shares the burdens with those who understand and who can share helpful ideas and insights. Barbara Deane says, "A Christian support group should be sensitive to participants' spiritual needs, give prayer support, and provide a ministry of encouragement."[1]

Many resources to help with the care of your loved ones were discussed in Chapter 10, and they will help you with your own physical and emotional needs. You cannot know if your caregiving responsibilities will go on for a week or a month or for many years, so it is important that you preserve your physical, mental and spiritual strength, not only for your loved ones and your family, but also for yourself.

———

While you are caregiving, it's easy to neglect yourself and focus solely on the person who needs your help. But this will only wear you out and negatively affect your relationship with your aging loved one. Be sure to take the time to refocus on your personal needs:

- Share the needs with others and solicit their help.
- Delegate responsibilities to lighten your load.
- Take time out to refresh your mind and body without guilt.
- Take time out for God.
- Use time spaces of each day productively.
- Use the available resources with no qualms.

12

Refocusing on Your Parents

W hen my mother and father died, the fact that the information regarding their backgrounds was gone came as a shock. We could no longer ask about grandparents or our heritage. Anything we'd been told would have to suffice unless we were fortunate enough to find another relative who could fill in the details.

Only hours after my father died, the funeral director asked me a question about him. My first reaction was to "ask Pop." It was then the reality hit me that I could no longer go to them with my questions.

The history of your parents is important, not only for posterity but to know who they are while they are still living. They may be old with gray hair and stooped bodies, but they are the aggregate of their lives, the products of their backgrounds, heritage, education and experiences. Instead of thinking of them from a one-dimensional perspective, begin to see them as complete human beings—physical, emotional, spiritual persons who think and act out of their backgrounds.

As I mentioned earlier, I was angry when people saw my folks only as old people ready to die. Mom and Dad weren't understood as whole people. If you talk to anyone at age forty, they will tell you that they don't feel any older than when they were twenty or thirty. People in their eighties or nineties, though their voices may quiver, have stories of marriage, childbirth, working conditions and struggles, just like people half their age. And often they will express the sorrow of losing a husband or wife, or a son in the war.

A lady in her nineties told me of her forty-year marriage and the death of her husband. Twenty-six years later, at the age of eighty-two, she remarried. Her nearly sightless eyes were teary as she told of her second husband's death only weeks earlier. Everyone had said she was foolish to marry at her age, she told me. But it was a fun marriage, she added with twinkling eyes. I put my arms around her and hugged her. "That's what I miss most about being a widow—not being hugged," she said.

I could relate many stories of aging loved ones, people whom I have come to know and love, who are old in years but not in soul or spirit. Perhaps no story says it more poignantly than when Nanny was in the board-and-care home.

Nanny was always an early riser, not one to "loll around in bed" in the morning hours. She was up and dressed and about her work, from her young years even to her oldest.

In the home were two other residents. One was an eighty-eight-year-old woman, the other a ninety-two-year-old man. The woman often didn't get dressed but went about all day in her slippers and robe over her nightie. Her white hair was usually in wild disarray. She sometimes went to sit with the elderly man who was flat in bed, unable to get up.

This incensed Nanny. To think of anyone running around in her "nightdress" was disgraceful enough—and she told the woman just that—but to sit in a man's bedroom clothed in that fashion was scandalous. "Why," Nanny exclaimed scornfully, "that old woman's man-crazy." Nanny was in her nineties, still young in her mind, and even a bit coy and flirtatious when a gentleman paid her attention.

Nanny, like all of us, was the total of her ninety years. I knew a great deal of her history from my mother and father, and from Nanny herself; consequently I understood many of her ways.

Sharing the Bond of Being Human

When we begin to see our loved ones from holistic and historical perspectives, they become more than just old people. They become real. They become interesting. They become examples in their aged wisdom. And they become more enjoyable to be with.

And just as our aging ones become more interesting to us when we know who they are, they respond to someone who cares about their earlier years. Usually they love telling and reviewing their lives. Maggie Kuhn, in her book, *Maggie Kuhn on Aging: A Dialogue by Dieter Hessel*, talks about "life review"—valuing the history, origin and experiences of the elderly. She says,

> If we could simulate a life review, we would see what we have lived through, the ways in which we have coped and survived, the changes we have seen—all of this is the history of the race. Older Americans have lived through more changes than any other human group.[1]

As well as learning about and appreciating our loved ones, it is also important that we share our lives with them. That is one way to keep them in touch and caring about others. If we exclude them, it is natural for them to turn inward and dwell on themselves and their problems.

My parents were vitally interested in our lives and what was happening with their grandchildren. They attended weddings and graduations and looked forward to visits from us and our children.

My father had a love for travel and a curiosity about new places. Even in the last month of his life he talked about flying to Alaska to see my son and the place where he lived and worked.

Both my son and daughter wrote letters to their grandparents sharing their experiences. Their Althens grandfather faithfully watched for the Alaska weather report, and he boasted about their accomplishments.

Sensitivity to our loved ones is a vital part of caregiving. As we begin to understand them, we learn more than caregiving; we learn how to grow old ourselves. We can put ourselves in their place and treat them as we would like to be treated. The Bible says: "Do unto others as you would have done to you" (Matthew 7:12). When we observe this Golden Rule of Life, treating our older family members with love, kindness, compassion and respect, we are fulfilling the law of God, to love others as we love ourselves.

Honoring Our Parents

One of the ways we can demonstrate our love is to let them be parents. Often we become independent and arrogant, giving our parents the message that they are not needed any longer. However, there are times when we should honor that relationship and heed their concerned counsel.

I gathered up the laundry one night to take to the laundromat. It was a balmy Florida evening, and I thought nothing of going after dark. But my mother and father both expressed concern for my safety. A week before, a woman had been accosted in the laundromat and her purse stolen. I argued that I would be fine, and I was perfectly able to take care of myself. In that instant the still small voice of God spoke to me about honoring my parents. What was more important: stubbornly going to the laundromat or giving them peace of mind? I realized the selfishness of causing them anxiety the entire time I was gone, not knowing if I would be safe and being helpless to do anything about it if I were not. The laundry didn't get done that night, and I learned an important lesson.

At times we forget that through a lifetime of making decisions they have learned wisdom, and we are wise when we ask their counsel occasionally. We may not heed their suggestions but they have perspectives that come from years of living.

When my father asked what we were going to do during those days in Florida, I would have been wise to ask his advice. I was wrong not to. He may not have been able to suggest anything, but it would have given him the opportunity to express his thoughts and feelings. Perhaps sharing the problems with Pop would have lessened my overwhelming burden, and it also may have relieved his feeling of helplessness somewhat. We need to respect our aging loved ones and treat them with the dignity they deserve.

Another area that merits consideration is personal care. The humiliation of aging bodies has been mentioned in other chapters. It is particularly difficult for our loved ones to relinquish their most intimate care to another person. They should be accorded the utmost respect for their modesty and privacy. This requires sensitivity and thoughtfulness and guarding against carelessly exposing them when caring for their needs.

While being bathed, they should be kept covered and warm, washing small areas at a time. If they are in a tub or shower, it is sometimes necessary to be close by, but they are much better off if they can take some of the responsibility for washing themselves, away from watchful eyes.

Caregivers can take control until every vestige of their loved ones' privacy is gone, but as husbands and wives our parents need privacy together. They need to talk alone as a couple, to love each other and to express their love in their own ways without interference.

We give our loved ones a sense of value and significance if we regard them with the same respect we expect from our children and others.

If we begin to see our loved ones not just as our parents but as human beings whose lives have had significance and meaning, who are loved by God who does not judge according to age, youth or beauty, then we are learning the secret of caregiving. The best caregiving comes from a heart of love, and is given as unto the Lord.

——

Have you noticed how your treatment of your aging loved ones has been recently? Do you consider them as loved human beings? Perhaps it's time to refocus on your loved ones:

- They are the total of their lives—background, culture, experience.
- Let them be parents occasionally.
- Seek their counsel.
- See them as complete human beings—physically, mentally and spiritually.
- Involve them in your lives.
- Encourage them to share their history.
- Learn from your loved ones how to grow old yourself.

13

Refocusing on Caregiving

Perhaps one of the easiest things to do as a caregiver is lose your perspective. After difficult periods you may become so caught up in your own world that you forget the true purpose of the task at hand. In this chapter we'll refocus on the job before you and present some tips on doing the best you can do as a caregiver.

The term "caregiving" implies safekeeping and protection, having a concern for a person's needs. The areas of care are physical, social and spiritual. How the needs are met makes a difference in the quality of life of another person.

Physical Care

Meeting our loved ones' physical needs is important for both their mental and physical energy. Good nutrition is essential for the prevention of diseases and for general good health.

My mother suffered from osteoporosis and painful arthritis. To a large extent, I blame her condition on her poor eating habits when she was younger. Mom had been an exceptionally strong woman physically. She was proud of her strong body, and I think she could not imagine that her strength would ever desert her.

Throughout her seven pregnancies there was little money with which to buy food. During the depression our family received "relief" through government food supplies—

powdered and evaporated milk, raisins and other foods. We planted a small garden and raised chickens. Mom made sure her children were fed with the best she could provide, but she wouldn't eat until my father and all of us had been fed. It was rare that she sat down to eat a meal with us, and I think she must have survived on leftovers. Her pregnancies and neglect of herself left her physically depleted, and the consequences were loss of her teeth and brittle bones.

Although life improved economically for my folks as they grew older, and Mom began to eat better as the children left home, the damage had been done. What she had lost could not be replaced.

J. Oswald Sanders says,

> Correct nutrition plays an important part in the maintenance of health in old age, and one helpful contribution is to enjoy one's food! The quality of diet in earlier years will have helped to determine our physical condition at this stage. Energy-producing foods such as carbohydrates are not needed in such quantities as earlier in life. The value of what are called primary foods—fruit, meat, fish, vegetables, whole grain cereals—should be recognized in the selection of diet. Elderly people should drink more rather than less than before . . . If the diet is reasonably well-balanced, fewer pills will be required. Eating small meals more frequently has been found helpful by some.

> As we grow older, the body burns up less fat in energy because we are less active than before . . . At the age of sixty-five it is generally held that one needs 20 percent fewer calories to maintain bodily functions than at twenty-five.[1]

Peggy Eastman quotes Dr. J. Michael McGinnis, Chairman of the Department of Health and Human Services Nutrition Policy Board, on the subject of nutrition:

> Common sense has always told us there was a strong link between diet and health. Now there is a solid and

growing base of scientific evidence which shows that a few key dietary changes can help prevent many of our most serious chronic diseases.

One of the report's key conclusions is that if you drink moderately and don't smoke, what you eat can influence long-term health more than any other action you might take.[2]

William P. Costelli, Director of the Framingham, Massachusetts Heart Study, wrote, "The rules for cholesterol should be tougher the older you get...You may not live longer, but you'll be less likely to have a heart attack prematurely. The quality of your life will be a whole lot better!"[3]

Referring to a study conducted by the Honolulu Heart Program, Dr. Basil Rifkind, head of cholesterol research of the National Heart, Lung and Blood Institute, says:

The study means that the elderly should pay more attention to their cholesterol, after all... By doing this, they will reduce their risk of heart disease.[4]

Former Surgeon General C. Everett Koop, in his report on nutritional health studies, agrees, stating that cutting down on foods high in saturated fats—butter, bacon, commercial baked goods—is of primary importance.[5]

Erik Erikson in *Vital Involvement in Old Age* says:

It would be wise and forward-looking for more medical professionals to focus their research on the prevention of those ailments of older people that are not essentially intrinsic to aging itself. Arthritis, heart disease, cataracts and ear defects, for example, are not necessarily due entirely to the aging process, although the lowered tonus of the body makes it more vulnerable to them. Both arthritis and heart disease may to some degree be checked by appropriate diet. Direct or constant glare, we are warned, induces cataracts, and some ear defects are caused by extremes of intensif d sound."[6]

Many aged ones who live alone tend to neglect their physical needs. Often they don't see well enough to prepare food, they lack motivation to cook for themselves and they find eating alone depressing. They need someone to shop for nutritious food that can be prepared easily, and someone to monitor their eating habits. Sometimes food spoils in the cupboard or refrigerator, and dishes aren't washed properly, so the possibility of illness exists. Good nutrition is a significant factor in maintaining the best possible health for our loved ones.

Exercise

A second essential for good health is exercise. Two government-sponsored agencies, the National Center for Nursing Research and the National Institute on Aging, are conducting a three-year project—Frailty and Injury: Cooperative Studies of Intervention Techniques. According to an article in *The Orange County Register*, the program "will include exercise, ranging from the Chinese martial art tai chi to aerobic dance; education to make older people aware of accident risks; and rehabilitation to improve physical conditioning."[7]

The article quotes Dr. T. Franklin Williams, the institute's director, who says, "The new trials highlight the fact that frailty and injuries are not the inevitable outcome of aging. Instead they are problems for which we have now found some very viable solutions."

Robin Henig, in an article on exercise for older persons, also quotes Dr. Williams in regard to exercise programs for the aging: "No matter how modest the routine and no matter how late in life it is begun, an exercise program can always have health benefits." In the same article, Harvard professor Alexander Leaf says, "Exercise is the closest thing we have to an anti-aging pill," and Dr. Lawrence Shulman, conference coordinator and director of the National Institute of Arthritis and Musculoskeletal Diseases, points out that the benefits of exercise can go beyond physical health: "Regular, faithful, intelligent exercise affords a sense of joy and achievement, of confidence and competence."[8]

Erikson says in *Vital Involvement in Old Age*, "Old bodies can be revitalized through appropriate exercise so that every movement involved in the day's activities can become a pleasure rather than a task."[9]

My earliest memories of my grandmother are of her walking from her house by the river to our farm on the other side of town, a distance of about two miles. She enjoyed berry-picking and would gather up her buckets and climb the hill to the woods and the blueberry patches. She would walk miles to find a thicket of blackberries or raspberries. After her buckets—and her straw hat—were filled, she would walk back to her house.

She also walked to town almost every day, to visit or do errands. Even in her eighties she had hardly slowed her pace. Nanny was a healthy woman until she died in her nineties, and I believe the many years of walking were largely responsible for her continued health and longevity.

Dr. Herbert de Vries, of the Gerontology Center of the University of Southern California, states:

> Walking [is] the best exercise for regaining vitality. It is the easiest way for an older person to obtain exercise, as it is so flexible. One can walk fast or slow; alone or in company; gently or vigorously; in the park or on the street; in summer and in winter. It calls for no skill and involves no equipment—except a walking stick. You can stop for a rest at will.[10]

Exercise is essential to good health.

Sleep

A third essential for good health and vitality is restful sleep and comfort. It is important that older people are warm, that bed covers are adequate but not too heavy, that pillows are comfortable and mattresses not too hard or soft, and that sheets are smooth and wrinkle-free. An irregularity in any one of these could result in sleeplessness.

My mother was concerned about my father's restlessness at night. He thrashed around, with the bed covers untucked and wadded up, and consequently he slept poorly. We decided to purchase a mattress warmer similar to the one on Mom's bed. That pad made a great difference. The bed was warm and comfortable, and my father began to sleep restfully.

Often our body temperature is just below the comfort level, and another blanket or the electric blanket turned up slightly will make the difference between sleep and wakefulness.

People seem to require fewer hours of sleep as they grow older. This may be due to less active days or more frequent naps.

One of the best inducements to sleep is a mind free from anxiety. Softly played music helped my parents relax. My daughter sent me a cassette she had made for them; on one side she sang scriptures she had set to music, and on the other psalms were set to music. When my folks were tucked in for the night, I turned on the cassette player so they could relax and fill their minds with beautiful thoughts. During my father's last days while he was in a coma, I played Lori's tape and hoped that if he could still hear, it would minister to his spirit.

Cleanliness

Another essential for a healthy attitude and self-esteem is cleanliness. We all know how we feel when we need to bathe or wash our hair. When our loved ones are unable to do this, they don't feel good about themselves; consequently their attitude is not positive or cheerful to those around them.

Our loved ones should be kept clean. Their hair should be shampooed regularly and arranged attractively. A shower or bath should be given as often as possible. Sometimes this might be a sponge bath while they are sitting in a chair or, if necessary, lying in bed. After the bath, they should be wiped dry and rubbed with lotion and powdered. A back rub is also very relaxing. They will feel good and smell fragrant. Their muscles will be stimulated by the washing, drying and applying of lotion.

Care of the feet is important too. My mother tended to our feet when we were children, massaging them and cutting our toenails, making sure there were no ingrown edges. I liked the way my feet felt after Mom did this.

Often the toenails of aged ones are difficult to cut. Special clippers are available for that purpose. My mother's toenails were tough and I didn't like to cut them because I was fearful of injuring her. Soaking the feet in warm soapy water before attempting the job helps to soften the nails. A friend of mine takes her ninety-year-old father to the podiatrist every two weeks.

Fingernails should also be kept trimmed and clean. The cuticles can be kept soft by applying Vaseline petroleum jelly at bedtime. Ragged or split nails can be a nuisance and can cause nail-biting. They also tend to catch on clothing.

Clothing
After a shampoo and bath, clean under and outer garments or nightclothes that are loose-fitting and soft against the skin will give your loved one comfort.

A clean bed, an attractive room that has been freshened by opening windows (while your loved one is out of the room), and a change of clothing will help your loved ones to relax and to know they have value.

Clothing of soft fabrics and pretty colors in attractive styles add to the dignity of a person. Age is no reason to give up bright colors. There is a unique beauty that belongs to our aged loved ones, and that beauty can be enhanced by our loving efforts to help them be as attractive as possible.

My sister Lee made pretty pantsuits for Mom of knit fabric with elasticized waists that were easy to pull on. The jackets buttoned up the front and could be worn with or without a blouse. My favorite was a deep rose suit that was especially attractive with Mom's softly curled white hair. It was a joy to see my mother and father clean, rested and well-dressed, just as they had been in their younger years.

The personal care essentials of nutrition, exercise, cleanliness and comfortable clothing can bolster the self-esteem of your parents. They will feel loved and cared for. They will feel they have significance. We can bring out the best in aged people when we make loving efforts to meet these basic needs and encourage them to look and feel their best for God.

Social Care

Besides the physical aspects of caregiving in keeping our loved ones mentally and physically healthy, the social aspect is also of great importance. Interaction with others helps to keep the elderly vitally alive and interested in people and in life. When people are isolated from contact with others, both young and old, and from events in the world around them, the tendency is to withdraw and become socially shriveled, no longer caring about self or anyone else.

Aging people need to be loved, hugged, touched and talked to. It is a lonesome time for them when others are repelled by their old bodies.

In Florida, my mother and father belonged to a community of people with various interests. In the quad lived a widow who walked bent nearly double due to a severe back problem. In her younger years she and her husband had been coal miners. Now she lived alone and spent her time working on projects for her family and for other people. She had turned her patio into a work area. Yards of material, her sewing machine and a large work table crowded the screened room where she designed and assembled the brilliant patches into colorful quilts and other projects. For years I had in my home a small stool made from fruit juice cans, padded and covered with pretty fabric, made by my mother with the help of this friend.

My mother had been isolated for years on the farm in New Hampshire while my father worked on his railroad job away from home. After the children were grown she was alone for days at a time. She didn't drive and her arthritis prevented her from walking very far, so she was limited in her social contacts with others.

In Florida there were other women to visit with, and they shared common family interests. Mom often visited with the "quilt lady," helping with her sewing and learning to make the small padded stools. It was a time of social growth and enjoyment for her after her years on the farm. Her interaction with the neighbors and in the church gave her many things to think and talk about.

Whenever I was in Florida I was welcomed warmly. In comparing my years with theirs, my parents' friends saw me as a youngster, and it rejuvenated them to visit with a younger person. I listened to their stories and their experiences. A lady in her nineties who had been a lawyer, graduating from a prestigious college, was in the process of writing a book. One of the ladies, a godly woman now in her eighties, became a treasured friend with whom I still keep in touch. My daughter, Lori, said she was fascinated by old people who had spent their years in godly living.

Erikson, in *Vital Involvement in Old Age*, says:

> Old people can derive great pleasure from being with younger men and women and can delight in the spontaneous playfulness of children ... It could well be claimed that the habitual peer grouping that is so impoverishing for the elderly is at the root of ageism that besets society today.[11]

The aged and the young seem to have an affinity for each other. Perhaps it is the trust and untarnished innocence of the child that sees through the wrinkled and stooped bodies to the heart, and maybe for the aged ones, the precious simplicity of the child evokes memories of their happy and carefree youth.

In an article, "And a Little Child Shall Lead Them," Mark Cutshall tells the story of Florence Turnidge taking her granddaughter to visit a man dying of cancer and creating a ministry of joy. Since that time other children have enriched the lives of aged residents through visiting that nursing home in Washington. The article quotes Florence:

> Often you can feel an immediate emotional bond between the kids and the elderly... There is something about children that brings new life and enthusiasm to [them].[12]

Nine-year-old Megan lived next door to me, and across the way lived Mabel, who was in her nineties. Megan delighted in visiting Mabel. Even though Mabel was unable to communicate verbally because of a stroke, Megan found ways to bring smiles to her face. She played games with Mabel, and brought flowers to her from the garden.

During the warm summer months Mabel sat with her feet in the wading pool while Megan splashed about entertaining and delighting her.

As I watched those two, the very old and the very young, I realized that neither age nor lack of verbal communication were barriers to their friendship. Each was giving something precious to the other.

Erikson talks about the advantage of involving the aged in creative activities and the benefits of the elderly participating in art, music, drama and writing. He says:

> Rather than leaving old people uninvolved with nothing to think about except their own deterioration, we should foster the delight and involvement of the senses in such a setting as a lively studio workshop... When young people—or any other generation, especially children—are also involved, the change in the mood of elders can be unmistakably vitalizing.[13]

There are many stories about elderly men and women in their seventies, eighties and even nineties who are proving that continued interaction with people and stimulating creative activities keep them interested in the world around them. As seventy-seven-year-old Joe Rubinger put it: "Ultimately, I hope that our segment of society, with our vast experience, will have enough political clout to greatly improve the lot of mankind."[14]

When the physical, emotional and social needs are met, the aging ones tend to stay intellectually alert, keeping abreast of national and community issues. They recognize that they are valuable contributors in society.

Mardy Murie is an example of one who doesn't consider age a detriment to her cause. She is "one of the country's influential champions of wildlife and wilderness areas." Eighty-eight years old, she has made her environmental message known in high places. She was among those who shared the stage when President Bush traveled to Jackson Hole to publicize one of his major environmental goals, a plan to strengthen the Clean Air Act. Of her efforts "to preserve the caribou calving area in the Alaskan refuge," and her keen interest in "putting the wolves back in Yellowstone" she says: "Whatever happens . . . it's more fun to be in the performance than to stand with your face to the wall."[15]

We need to encourage our aged ones to share their experiences and participate as much as possible. If participation is impossible, it is important to help them be aware of the news and what's going on in the world around them. Encourage loved ones to have their own opinions, and then don't discourage their verbal responses to events. My friend Dona maintains that this is helping to keep her infirm mother independent, and she respects her mother's ideas and views.

It is important to encourage our aged ones to use their minds and to not shut them out when they express their views. Many younger people are intolerant and impatient with the older perspective, not hearing the wisdom of years of experience. Even if the aged don't have pearls of wisdom to offer, they are entitled to their views and the right to express them.

If your loved one is unable to read because of poor eyesight, you can get "talking books" and newspapers and magazines on cassette at almost any library. As an option, a few minutes each week could be spent in recording news items on your loved one's favorite subject or humorous stories from books or magazines. These tapes would give your aged ones hours of pleasure—and you, the caregiver, a more rewarding job. There is no limit to the creative ways you can keep your loved ones intellectually alert and interesting.

Spiritual Care

The last, but by no means least, area to be met in the lives of your loved ones is spiritual. As mentioned in an earlier chapter, every person is a total being with physical, emotional and spiritual needs. If the needs of one of these areas go unmet, the whole body suffers. Therefore, meeting the spiritual needs of your loved ones will make a difference in their overall health.

Judith Shelly and Sharon Fish, in their book *Spiritual Care, The Nurse's Role*, say:

> Our nursing care must be focused on the person as a unity. The key to human integration is a relationship with God which permeates the whole being. Through a relationship with God, we find our worth and identity and become free to love and be loved by others . . . Life draws its definition and finds its meaning and worth from its source. A Christian believes that God is the source of all life; our concept of humanity therefore reflects that belief.[16]

During the month I cared for my folks in Florida, I took them to the little chapel close by. They enjoyed the sermons and the singing. Many times we talked about the message on the way home. Although my father wasn't able to articulate well, he would say with emphatic nods, "Good sermon."

The pastor visited their home, and that strengthened and blessed them. There is always a need for fellowship, and we can encourage that fellowship by inviting others from the church to visit.

At bedtime I read the Scriptures to them, sitting on my father's bed. He especially liked the book of Joshua. After reading I knelt between their beds holding their hands and prayed, then played my daughter's tape of scriptural songs. I believe this helped to comfort and settle them for a more restful sleep.

My father wasn't one to talk about his faith. He was from Yankee stock who kept "religious" views private. Consequently, I didn't know if he knew Jesus Christ in a personal way. But one day while I was washing dishes, my father sat quietly watching me.

Suddenly he said, "I've got it all together with Him." I turned to look at him.

"Who, Pop?" I asked. He raised his stiff right arm and pointed upward. "Jesus Christ," he said in his garbled way. "He died on the cross for my sins. He's my Savior."

I felt the tears starting, and I wanted to rush to him and throw my arms around him. Instead I told him I was happy to hear that news. I feel he told me because of all that had happened during the years of concern for him. Hearing my father tell me that he knew Jesus Christ was a never-to-be-forgotten blessing of caring for my folks, one I could share with my brothers and sisters.

Another spiritual blessing during those last days was the privilege of praying with my mother. She was a devout woman throughout her lifetime, but because unkind people ridiculed her, her faith went "underground." She rarely talked about the Lord. One night she sat in her bed, her head bowed. When I walked into the room she looked up and asked, "Would you pray with me?" I sat down on her bed and held her hands as we prayed and cried together.

Spiritual care must be given with love and kindness. I continued to learn more of this as my caregiving went on. Our loved ones are facing death, and there is no peace without the indwelling presence of the Holy Spirit in their lives.

Although spiritual care is important to our loved ones, it is only as effective as our own personal relationship with God. All that we have to give our loved ones has its source in God in the person of Jesus Christ. It is He who gives us the strength, love and grace to do our task.

———

I hope I've encouraged you in your caregiving task. As you go about your day-to-day duties, be sure to allow time to refocus on the caregiving of your loved ones:

- Physical needs are important to well-being and self-esteem—diet, exercise, rest, cleanliness, beauty.

- Social activity keeps loved ones alert to life.

- Isolation or contact with only the elderly can cause withdrawal.

- Young people can help aging ones stay alert and involved.

- Encourage aging ones to be involved in life, to use their minds.

- Fulfilled spiritual needs result in peace and acceptance of life and hope in death.

14

Refocusing on the Joy

A mong the weighty responsibilities of caregiving, along with the demands and frustrations of our situation, amid the sadness and grief of the aging process, we all have moments of joy. There are times when we smile and laugh and create some happy memories with our aging loved ones.

As caregivers, we make the lives of our aged ones more enjoyable when we strive to lighten their lives with things they can think on and talk about in the days that follow. And we also learn more about our loved ones during these activities, things we might never know otherwise.

When my mother was in the hospital with congestive heart failure, I brought her a single yellow rose in a vase. She exclaimed, "Oh, yellow roses have always been my favorite." I didn't know that. She had never told anyone that I know of, but with this simple gesture I learned a little more about Mom.

Giving Special Tokens of Your Love

In my family we have a word to describe gifts and little things given for no particular reason. That word is "sprizie." A sprizie is a "just because I love you" present. It can be the tiniest and least expensive of gifts, but it brings joy and pleasure. A favorite candy bar or a can of peanuts were some sprizies my folks enjoyed. Other suggestions are a bouquet of flowers, a book, a tape of grandchildren talking and laughing.

There is no end to the creative sprizies your aged ones might enjoy. Sprizies don't have to be practical or edible or usable—a pretty stone or a crystal to catch the rays of the sun. Whatever brings pleasure to your aged ones is certain to bring even greater joy to you, the caregiver. Everyone benefits from giving. Your loved ones gain a feeling of worth along with the pleasure of receiving, and you, the warm glow of being the giver of love and joy.

One caregiver shared the story of taking her mother for a ride in a limousine. The limousine came to the house, picked her up and drove her through the town. Her mom was thrilled and said, "I never expected to ride in a limousine until I was dead."

Another caregiver took her mother to the beauty shop every week for a manicure and an occasional pedicure. In addition to having her nails well-groomed, the personal attention made her loved one feel special. Everyone at the beauty shop loved her and looked forward to her coming. She enjoyed talking with the attendants and sharing stories of herself. Socially and physically she benefited from the thoughtfulness of her daughter.

My friend Shirley told me her story. She sat in a hospital waiting room in Hawaii while her mom lay in a coma in the Intensive Care Unit. The doctor told her that her mother did not have long to live. Her vital signs were not consistent with life; her kidneys had failed and her blood pressure barely registered. Shirley heard what he said and did not respond. The doctor, thinking she had not understood, repeated his conclusions. "Do you understand what I've told you?" he asked.

Shirley said simply, "My mother is dying. I'd like to be with her."

Shirley's mother had longed to take a trip to Hawaii for many years and finally she and Shirley were able to go. It was worth every minute to Shirley to see the pleasure of anticipation and the thrill of reality as her mom first saw the beautiful and fragrant island. They had enjoyed almost a week together before she became ill. Shirley concluded that if God ordained the death of her mom there in Hawaii, it was a fitting conclusion to a lifelong dream.

Shirley's mother didn't die there but recovered sufficiently to fly home and enjoy several more months with her family around her.

The trip to Hawaii was not a trial to be borne by Shirley but a memory to savor, even with her mother's illness. We can't all take our loved ones on trips to Hawaii, but whatever we do is making a memory for the future, and joy for the remainder of the life of our loved one. Shirley's mom took great pleasure in reliving her experiences and sharing this dream-come-true with others.

Cheryl, who cared for her mom in her home, shared her memories with me:

> Our last big outing together was shopping at the mall. Actually she was fulfilling a request her mother made of her: My grandma, who had been gone more than two years, had asked my mom to buy me some good china ... Mom and I walked the entire Westminster Mall to be sure it was what I wanted. I think deep in her soul she knew time was short, and there was an appropriate "sale." I felt the need to cherish that evening's experience because I knew it was one of our last. When the china arrived my mom was so proud of it, and she insisted that all her visitors see it.

> After her death it was very difficult to use those dishes but now it makes me happy and I enjoy entertaining company with my beautiful "good china."

Spending Time in "History"
Whether old or young, people need to sense that they still have worth, and that their lives have had significance. Much

of that value and significance comes from sharing their experiences with others and being listened to. As caregivers we are privy to some of our greatest lessons in history. But it is easy to think that we have all the answers in our youthful maturity, and we forget to listen.

In *Learn to Grow Old*, Paul Tournier speaks about the uniqueness of the mind of the aged, and the importance of listening to them:

> Behind the unchanging facade there is a mind—a mind that lives, a mind that suffers and feels pleasure, a mind that thinks and feels. It is a mind fashioned by the multitudinous experiences of a long life, its successes and failures, its joys and disappointments . . . They hide this unique mind of theirs because they feel that no one is interested in it, because they think that what they could say about their lives is of no interest to anyone, because they do not feel themselves to be loved . . .

> Maybe you will work a miracle of love if you persevere, if you talk to them in a way that is really personal, if you engage in the dialogue with your most intimate thoughts on life . . . And then, listen to them; listen to them with attention and love . . . Then listen to these old people in order to learn what life is, from the mouths of those who have lived it fully.[1]

My mother's parents were immigrants from Germany, and it is a story that one day I want to tell. She told of her peasant mother and aristocrat father meeting and marrying in America against all the traditions of the "old country." The telling of this fascinating tale gave my mother identity and distinction. I wish I had listened more closely. Much was lost of the history and the experiences of my parents—important facts about my heritage that are now unavailable to me and to my children and grandchildren.

Florence Littauer, in her book *Your Personality Tree*, tells the story of her mother-in-law, and how, in a "rare moment of disclosure," Florence discovered a person she'd never known in all the years she had been married:

> I encouraged [my mother-in-law] to tell me how she really felt, and she shared one heartbreaking story.
>
> She was in love with a young man while at Cornell and they had talked of marriage. Her mother disapproved because she felt he did not come from an important or wealthy enough family. After college they went in separate directions for the summer, and he was to call her in the fall. She never heard from him again.
>
> At the mention of this fact, this beautiful woman burst into tears, and I thought the sad story was over. I'd never seen her let down her guard before, and I felt so sorry for how this rejection still bothered her. As I sat quietly, wondering what I should say, she looked up and continued. "That's not the end of it. I went to a party just a few years ago and there he was. I found out he was a successful lawyer, and then I asked that question, 'Why didn't you ever call me?'
>
> " 'Oh, I called all right,' he replied. 'I talked to your mother on the telephone, and she told me that you were engaged to another man, that you didn't love me, and that you'd asked her to tell me never to call again.' "
>
> Mother's ample frame shook as she sobbed out these last words. I knelt beside her and felt a warmth and compassion for her I'd never known before. How seldom we sense what's stored up inside a person just waiting for a quiet moment, a nonthreatening situation to be set free.

Florence encouraged her mother-in-law to continue talking. She heard of Mother Littauer's desire to be an opera singer, and how it had been thwarted by her parents as a "waste of time."

[Mother] got up quickly, went to a closet and pulled out a box of old pictures. She showed me a large photo of a stage setting with a cast posed for review. "There I am." She pointed proudly to a confident and beautiful young girl seated on an ornate chair, center stage, the obvious star of the show.

At the end of this memorable and meaningful evening, Mother gave me the picture of her on stage in her one starring role, and I treasure this memory of what might have been.[2]

As we encourage our loved ones to reminisce, and we listen to them, writing or taping conversations, we will find a new joy in their lives and in our own as well.

Making the Final Memories the Best

These are the last times with our loved ones. Make them as happy and relaxed as possible. Brew a pot of tea and serve it in china cups, sit on the porch with them or beside their beds. Wheel them in their wheelchairs, or walk slowly beside them with their walkers. Point out the flowers and birds, the children, the animals. Help them to use their senses—to taste and touch, to smell the flowers on a fine spring day, to hear as much as possible, to see even in their mind's eye—to continue to experience life as God created it, and to focus on the joy instead of the despair that has permeated our lives.

Bring them a puppy or a kitten to pet, flowers to smell, or fragrance to wear. We are limited only by our own creativity in the ways to bring joy to our loved ones. However we choose to give love and joy to our aged ones, we are reflecting the love of God. Jesus said in Matthew 25:40, "Truly I say to you, to the extent that you did it to one of these brothers of Mine, even the least of them, you did it to Me" (NASB).

Instead of focusing on the dread and despair of our loved ones, focus on the joy. This will reap not only eternal rewards, but it will also grant a fuller, more complete life for them. It will teach us the value of age and give us a broader perspective in our own old age. We will be glad for the memories of doing all we could to make their lives rich until the end.

———

I know how the chore of caregiving can get, tiring and frustrating. When you feel like you've come to the end of your rope, that's the time to take a breather and refocus on the joy of caring for your loved ones:

- Be creative in bringing joy to your loved ones.
- Concentrate on the joy and blessings rather than the negatives.
- Encourage your loved ones to share their stories and listen to them.
- Bring them "sprizies."
- Make memories for them and for you.
- Make your time together relaxed and happy.

15

Refocusing on God's Perspective of Aging Ones

We have contemplated old age from the vantage point of the caregiver and our aged loved ones, but the final perspective comes from the Creator of life, God Himself. "It is He who has made us and not we ourselves" (Psalm 100:3). Is there any time of life that isn't important to God? Does He place more value on a child or young adult than on an aged one?

God places value on *all* human life. He has created us in His image for fellowship with Himself, and finally to be with Him for eternity. The love of God is all-encompassing; therefore we have the responsibility to view life as a God-given gift from birth to old age and death.

The fifth commandment instructs us to honor our mothers and fathers. This command doesn't expire when we become adults or get married, but extends all the way into our parents' old age. We show that honor by giving our loved ones respect and loving care.

My mother said to me, "If anyone is unkind to you I will take it up with the Lord!" Perhaps there is more to that statement than loving sentiments because the Lord has said, "That it may be well with you, and that you may live

long on the earth" (Ephesians 6:3). God did not say it would
be an effortless road to travel, but as we endeavor to obey
His commands He gives His coping power and the promise
of His blessings.

From the first, mothers and fathers were the pivot point
of life and stability in the family plan of God. They brought
forth life and nurtured it, guarding it with love, prayers and
work. And when the life-giving process is finished, it passes
into another stage, that of supporting through love and
prayers and encouragement.

My mother in rare moments would express how useless
she felt, that she was unable to do anything for us. My
answer to her was that in her years of "uselessness" she was
perhaps most helpful to us because of her prayers and
strong faith in the Lord. God didn't plan for us to be useless
at any stage of our adult lives.

Honoring God's Command

Mothers and fathers deserve to be honored as God has
commanded. Perhaps what we have experienced at their
hands influences our feelings toward our aging parents, but
God's command isn't conditional on our feelings or their
actions. We must obey His commands and let Him be the
judge of any unrighteous actions. There were no perfect
parents in the Bible, but it was God who brought judgment
against them, not the children.

Eli's sons Hophni and Phinehas were disobedient and
disrespectful to their father. He hadn't disciplined or trained
them in the ways of righteousness, and the Bible says, "They
would not listen to the voice of their father" (1 Samuel 2:25).
But it was God who put them to death and dealt sternly with
Eli.

The opposite of honor is found in Proverbs 20:20: "He
who curses his father or his mother, his lamp will go out in
time of darkness."

Matthew Henry's Commentary says:

An undutiful child becomes very wicked by degrees. He began with despising his father and mother, slighting their instructions, disobeying their commands, and raging at their rebukes, but at length he arrives at such impudence and impiety as to curse them...and to wish mischief to those who were the instrument of their being and have taken so much care and pains about him, and this in defiance to God's law...in violation of all the bonds of duty, natural affection, and gratitude.[1]

The dire result of such behavior is that "his lamp will go out in time of darkness." Rather than the promised well-being of obeying God's command to honor father and mother, the child will experience lack of peace and comfort in his life, especially as he travels the road into old age. God's commands are written, not only for the comfort and care of the aged ones, but also for the emotional well-being of children.

Following the Biblical Example

The book of Ruth is an example to us of caring for our aged loved ones. Naomi was an old woman, weighed down by the sorrows of losing her husband and two sons. Her only comfort seemed to be in returning to the land and home she'd been away from for so long. She was depressed, not understanding why God had dealt so bitterly with her.

But Ruth loved her mother-in-law who apparently was a kind and godly woman. She loved her enough to leave her own country and people to follow her, not only to her land but also to her God. She worked to support her mother-in-law and herself by gleaning in the fields. She listened to the counsel of Naomi and confided in her as her relationship with Boaz progressed.

> And when she came to her mother-in-law, she said,
> "How did it go, my daughter?" And she told her all that
> the man had done for her . . . Then she [Naomi] said,
> "Wait, my daughter, until you know how the matter
> turns out; for the man will not rest until he has settled
> it today" (Ruth 3:16,18).

Ruth honored Naomi in every sense of the word, and
when she married Boaz, Naomi was cared for by a loving
family and blessed with a grandchild.

The women in the village said to Naomi and Ruth,

> Blessed is the LORD who has not left you without a
> redeemer today, and may his name become famous in
> Israel. May he also be to you a restorer of life and a
> sustainer of your old age; for your daughter-in-law,
> who loves you and is better to you than seven sons, has
> given birth to him (Ruth 4:14,15).

Ruth obeyed God's commandment to honor her mother,
and God fulfilled His promise that it would be well with her.
Through Ruth's obedience, God used her in His plan to
begin the line of David.

God's Plans for Old Age

God often used aged people to do His work and carry out His
plan. He didn't put them aside because of their youthful
indiscretions, but trained them to be usable in their old age.
He tested them and strengthened their faith until they had
attained a level of maturity where they could bear the weight
of God's assignment for them.

Moses grew up in a rich man's palace with all the
luxuries afforded a son of Pharaoh. He was no doubt spoiled
by attention and material possessions. Yet he was an Is-
raelite, with a burden for his kinfolk who were suffering at
the hands of the Egyptians. In his youthful zeal he took
matters into his own hands to deliver one of his own out of

the hands of an Egyptian, and "he struck down the Egyptian and hid him in the sand" (Exodus 2:12). But it wasn't yet God's time to deliver His children through Moses, so He sent him away to tend sheep in mountainous Midian for the next forty years.

Moses was an old man when God called him at the burning bush and commissioned him to deliver the children of Israel out of the hand of Pharaoh. Moses had matured from that overzealous youth to a man of humble and tenacious faith. God could have used a younger man but He chose to use the aging Moses.

When God made the promise of a son to Abraham and Sarah, they were still in their reproductive years. They could have had a son by natural happenings, but God chose to wait until Abraham was ninety-nine years old and Sarah ninety, long past the years of procreation, for Isaac to be born. Even when they took matters into their own hands and produced Ishmael by a servant girl in their impatience, God didn't forget His promise.

When the ultimate test came, and God demanded deliberate obedience from Abraham in the sacrifice of Isaac, Abraham had the wisdom of age and also a tenacious faith.

Isaac could have refused to go with Abraham to Mount Moriah. After all, his father was an old man going up the mountain to sacrifice to God, and he didn't even have a lamb to sacrifice. But he listened to his father, and he inherited the promises that God had made to Abraham. Proverbs 23:22 says: "Listen to your father who begat you, and do not despise your mother when she is old."

God has a purpose for every stage of life, and with these stages come responsibilities. In the aged, the experiences of life with its sorrows, distresses and joys are valuable inasmuch as they have resulted in wisdom and greater knowledge and grace of God. This wisdom and knowledge is then used to teach and train the younger generation. Titus 2:2–8 instructs older men and women in their responsibilities to younger men and women:

> Older men are to be temperate, dignified, sensible, sound in faith, in love, in perseverance.

> Older women likewise are to be reverent in their behavior, not malicious gossips, not enslaved to much wine, teaching what is good, that they may encourage the young women to love their husbands, to love their children, to be sensible, pure, workers at home, kind, being subject to their own husbands, that the word of God may not be dishonored.

> Likewise urge the young men to be sensible; in all things show yourself to be an example of good deeds, with purity in doctrine, dignified, sound in speech which is beyond reproach, in order that the opponent may be put to shame, having nothing bad to say about us.

God places value on old age just as He does on every phase of life, and in each stage He continues to carry out His unique purpose and plan. Old age is significant to God, and it carries responsibility with it. We as caregivers have an obligation to obey God in His assignment, to care for our aged loved ones in such a way that His purpose for them can be carried out to the fullest extent.

———

It's good to remember that God has a special plan for everyone—no matter what stage of life they are in. Refocus on God's view of your aged loved ones:

- God places value on old age as He does on every stage of life.

- God has commanded us to honor our mothers and fathers.

- God has promised that it will be well for those who obey His commandment.

- God has given instructions and examples in His Word to guide our behavior toward aged ones.

Epilogue

When Your Loved Ones Are Gone

D eath of our loved ones is inevitable. Our grief, though, may have begun long before their death, and dealing with grief commences before the fact.

My grief began when I saw my dynamic parents trapped in decrepit, malfunctioning bodies. Their aged condition made me angry, and anger is one of the characteristics of grief. I wanted my folks to stay young in mind and body, and I was disappointed. I was angry not only at old age, but also at God who controlled life. Old age, I felt, was a cruel joke on life. It was a poor finale for living, working, raising children and being faithful.

But God, in His mercy, gave us a way of escape from this transitory life. We are not condemned to live forever in a corrupt world. Sorrow and suffering are daily trials exacting their toll on us mentally and physically, but we move on to be with Him in eternity where new bodies clothe our souls. The old shell is discarded, somewhat as a reptile sheds its old skin, in preparation for the new.

Old age is the last stage of life and the final scene is death. We try to deny it, or ignore it, or pretend it can't happen to our loved ones or to us. We know it happens to others, but it shocks us when it invades our lives. However, when death is accepted as part of God's plan for life, the sorrow of loss and separation, though still intense, is lifted by the reality of the hope in God.

During the last hours of my first husband's life, I talked
to him, but he was beyond human communication. When
my father lay dying in a coma, he was separated from our
human thoughts, reasonings and ministrations. Both my
husband and my father were in the final process of shedding
their outer shells for the fuller life of eternity with God in
Christ Jesus.

Steps to Dealing With Grief

As caregivers we begin to deal with grief by understanding
that our actions and attitudes toward those we care for will
affect our grief. Guilt, whether true or false, causes us to
lament our shortcomings and inadequacies. We thrash ourselves with the question "Why didn't we . . . ?" and with the
ever-present "If only . . . " In guilt we blame ourselves.

Guilt and anger go hand in hand in the process of grief,
and when turned inward they cause depression. Author R.
Scott Sullender says that we deal with these emotions by
acknowledging the anger whether it is toward ourselves or
others, and by expressing that anger and clarifying its
target.[1]

While anger, guilt and depression play a big part in the
process of grief, forgiveness plays an even greater part in
healing. Problems that have become internalized cause us
to develop attitudes toward our loved ones as well as ourselves. And even when the loved ones are gone, the problems
still remain. They are free but we are tormented. Only
forgiveness of our loved ones and ourselves will free us from
the self-inflicted punishment of memories. If we understand
that God's forgiveness through Jesus Christ is the answer
to our anger, guilt and grief, it will help the healing process.

Death leaves a void that cannot be filled by anyone else.
It doesn't matter how many people surround us and care for
us, the person who impacted our lives will always be part of
our emotional being. The loss, the emotional amputation,
leaves a painful, bleeding wound. But like most wounds,
healing takes place with proper care.

When a wound is fresh, we are constantly aware of it. We can hardly think of anything else. And so we talk about our wound. After my mother and father died, I seemed to talk of nothing else. It was almost a compulsion to talk about their deaths in every detail. Those last days and months were relived many times. My mind couldn't grasp the reality that they were gone, and talking was a catharsis. It cleansed me and eased my sorrow when I shared my thoughts and feelings. Then the sharing brought the reality of the separation and loss, and the wound began to heal. I knew healing was taking place when there was no longer the necessity to talk about my grief.

It is important to listen to people who are grieving. Many times we are afraid we won't know what to say or how to respond, but it isn't necessary to say anything. The significant thing is to listen attentively and love that grieving person.

The day following my first husband's death, I was alone in my hospital room. I started to cry, and my cries became uncontrollable sobs. Quietly a nurse slipped in, closed the door and sat beside me on the bed. She took my hand and listened as I sobbed out my grief, and her tears fell silently in sympathy with mine. She was there, not to give me answers, but to set me on the long road to recovery. Tears are the soothing balm of pain.

Paradoxically, laughter is a lifter and healer too. Like yeast that leavens bread, it lightens the heaviness of grief. And it is a gift from God just as the tears are.

As I wrote in an earlier chapter, the night before my mother died we stood around her bed with the pastor. We talked of many things and we laughed. It may have seemed out of place to some in that somber situation, anticipating Mom's death, and though it didn't alleviate the sadness we were experiencing, it did lighten the heavy burden of it. The Word of God says, "The Lord is near to the brokenhearted, and saves those who are crushed in spirit" (Psalm 34:18, NASB).

Spending Time With the Memories

How often my family has wished we had known our loved ones in their earlier years. My sisters and I opened "the trunk," which was filled with mystery while we were growing up. Whatever was dear to my mother was in that trunk. Among the things we found were letters written by Mom's sister from faraway places, a kimono sent as a gift, a baby's sweater and bonnet, and a portfolio of charcoal drawings. We saw Mom, a young woman, a talented artist, whose abilities became lost in the demands of life. We pictured a new mother cuddling her firstborn, warmed and wrapped in the now moth-eaten sweater, and we felt the loneliness of a woman longing for the sweet friendship of a beloved sister.

In the "camp chest" were a bag of marbles, and a baseball uniform complete with shin guards and catcher's mask. A catcher's mitt, worn out by the speed ball of a pitcher. Wordless reminders of younger years. Many things whispered in the silence, "This is who we were."

Before I left my mother's room for the last time, I took her things from the drawers. I thought of the suffering and deprivation she had endured during her lifetime, and it all lost importance in the light of eternity. What she and my father left of value was as intangible as a breeze, and only God knows where it blew and who it touched.

Going through the lifetime accumulations of a mother and father is a time-consuming task. Sentiment and practicality vie with each other, and decisions are necessary but wrenching.

Possessions are an ongoing part of life after death. They need to be dealt with at the appropriate time with the realization that earthly goods, however precious, belong to the earth.

Grief is a painful process. There is no way to shortcut it. It is a tunnel we must go through, but we know there is a light at the end. From the onset of grief to the final disbursement of possessions, we place experiences like footsteps along the road of life, and we eventually find a new reality that shapes itself around the once-open wound. Though the scar remains, the pain of the wound becomes a memory.

———

As caregivers we know that sooner or later the inevitable will happen and our loved ones will die. While you've probably begun the grieving process in your final days of caregiving, death will bring a new sadness. When your loved ones are gone:

- Recognize grief as a painful process that is lived through step by step.
- Acknowledge and deal with your anger, guilt, depression and unforgiveness.
- Accept your feelings as normal. Every person has the right to feel his or her own feelings.
- Talk about your loss, and allow others to talk about theirs.
- Let the tears flow. They are healing.
- Don't be afraid or ashamed of laughter within your grief.
- Accept age as a stage of life, with death as the exit and the entrance to eternal life.
- Disburse possessions at the appropriate time recognizing that they are earthly goods.
- Discover who your loved ones have been by what they have left behind.
- Memories are a precious gift from the Lord. Cherish and use them to encourage you along the road of life.
- Focus on the hope we have been given by God through His Son Jesus Christ.

Bibliography

—

"Ann Landers," *Los Angeles Times* (February 16, 1988).

Coleman, Barbara. "New Guide Focuses on Nursing Home Quality," *AARP News Bulletin* (November 1988).

Coleman, Barbara. "The Gentle Warriors," *AARP News Bulletin* (July/August 1988).

Crabb, Larry. *Basic Principles of Biblical Counseling* (Grand Rapids: Zondervan, 1975).

Cutshall, Mark. "And a Little Child Shall Lead Them," *Focus On the Family* (March 1989).

Deane, Barbara. *Caring for Your Aging Parents: When Love Is Not Enough* (Colorado Springs: NavPress, 1989).

Demkovich, Linda. "The Brain Game," *AARP News Bulletin* (May 1989).

Douglass, Richard L. *Domestic Mistreatment of the Elderly—Towards Prevention* (AARP, 1987).

Eastman, Peggy. "A Carrot a Day. . . ," *AARP News Bulletin* (November 1988).

Erikson, Erik H.; Erikson, Joan M.; and Kivnick, Helen Q. *Vital Involvement in Old Age* (New York: W. W. Norton & Co., Inc., 1986).

"For Joe, So Much to Learn," *AARP News Bulletin* (October 1989).

Henig, Robin Marantz. "Fear of Falling," *AARP News Bulletin* (April 1989).

Henry, Matthew. *Matthew Henry Commentary*, III (McLean, VA: MacDonald Publishing Co., n.d.).

Kessler, Nancy. "All for the Wild," *AARP News Bulletin* (October 1989).

Kiester, Edwin, Jr. "Stretched to the Limit," *50 Plus* (October 1988).

Kuhn, Maggie. *Maggie Kuhn on Aging: A Dialogue by Dieter Hessel* (Philadelphia: Westminster Press, 1977).

Littauer, Florence. *Personality Plus* (Old Tappan, NJ: Fleming H. Revell Co., 1983).

Littauer, Florence. *Your Personality Tree* (Dallas: Word Books, 1986).

McLeod, Don. "Abuse Abounds," *AARP News Bulletin* (May 1990).

"Nursing Homes Need Kindly Hands," *Modern Maturity* (December 1989–January 1990).

Sanders, J. Oswald. *Your Best Years* (Chicago: Moody Press, 1982).

Shelly, Judith Allen and Fish, Sharon. *Spiritual Care, The Nurse's Role,* Third Edition (Downers Grove: InterVarsity Press, 1988).

Siegel, Mark A.; Jacobs, Nancy R.; and Foster, Carol D., eds. *Domestic Violence No Longer Behind the Curtains* (Wylie, TX: Information Plus, 1989).

Siegel, Mark A. and Jacobs, Nancy R., eds. *Growing Old in America* (Plano: Instructional Aides, Inc., 1982).

Simon, Cheryl. "A Care Package," *Psychology Today* (April 1988).

Strokes: A Guide for the Family (Dallas: The American Heart Association National Center).

Subak-Sharpe, Genell J. and MacLean, Helene. "Prime of Life," *Family Circle Magazine* (January 10, 1989).

Sullender, R. Scott. *Grief and Growth* (Mahwah, NJ: Paulist Press, 1985).

"Three-Year Project to Focus on Frailty," *Orange County Register* (April 6, 1990).

Tournier, Paul. *Learn to Grow Old* (New York: Harper & Row, 1972).

Tournier, Paul. *The Healing of Persons* (New York: Harper
& Row Publications, 1965).

Von Brook, Patricia; Siegel, Mark A.; and Jacobs, Nancy
R., eds. *Growing Old in America*, The Information
Series on Current Topics (Wylie, TX: Information Plus,
1990).

Other Books to Help and Encourage

L'Engle, Madeleine. *The Summer of the Great Grandmother*
(New York: Farrar, Strauss and Giroux, 1974).

Skogland, Elizabeth. *A Divine Blessing* (Minneapolis:
World Wide Publications, 1988).

Stafford, Tim. *As Our Years Increase* (Grand Rapids:
Zondervan Publishing House, 1989).

Notes

—

Chapter 1

1. Edwin Kiester, Jr., "Stretched to the Limit," *50 Plus* (October 1988), p. 65.

Chapter 3

1. Paul Tournier, *Learn to Grow Old* (New York: Harper & Row Publications, Inc., 1972), p. 40. Reprinted by permission.
2. Erik H. Erikson, Joan M. Erikson, and Helen Q. Kivnick, *Vital Involvement in Old Age* (New York: W. W. Norton & Co., Inc., 1986), p. 301. Reprinted by permission.
3. Mark A. Siegel and Nancy R. Jacobs, eds. *Growing Old In America* (Plano, TX: Instructional Aides, Inc., 1982), p. 45.
4. Edwin Kiester, Jr., "Stretched to the Limit," *50 Plus* (October 1988), p. 66.

Chapter 4

1. Larry Crabb, *Basic Principles of Biblical Counseling* (Grand Rapids: Zondervan, 1975), p. 46.
2. Edwin Kiester, Jr., "Stretched to the Limit," *50 Plus* (October 1988), p. 67.

Chapter 5

1. "Ann Landers," *Los Angeles Times* (February 16, 1988). Reprinted by permission from Ann Landers and Creators Syndicate.
2. Erik H. Erikson, Joan M. Erikson, and Helen Q. Kivnick, *Vital Involvement in Old Age* (New York: W. W. Norton & Co., Inc., 1986), p. 200. Reprinted by permission.
3. Patricia Von Brook, Mark A. Siegel, and Nancy R. Jacobs, eds. *Growing Old in America*, The Information Series on Current Topics (Wylie, TX: Information Plus, 1990), p. 82.
4. Von Brook, et al, *Growing Old in America*, p. 83.

Chapter 6
1. Florence Littauer, *Personality Plus* (Old Tappan: Fleming H. Revell Co., 1983), p. 12.
2. Paul Tournier, *The Healing of Persons* (New York: Harper & Row, 1965), p. 76.
3. Barbara Deane, *Caring for Your Aging Parents: When Love Is Not Enough* (Colorado Springs: NavPress, 1989), p. 49.

Chapter 7
1. "Strokes: A Guide for the Family." Reprinted by permission of The American Heart Association of Tucson, Arizona.
2. Mark A. Siegel and Nancy R. Jacobs, eds. *Growing Old in America* (Plano: Instructional Aides, Inc., 1982), p. 34.
3. Linda Demkovich, "The Brain Game," *AARP News Bulletin* (May 1989).

Chapter 8
1. Robin Marantz Henig, "Fear of Falling," *AARP News Bulletin* (April 1989).
2. Genell J. Subak-Sharpe and Helene MacLean, "Prime of Life," *Family Circle Magazine* (January 10, 1989), p. 58.
3. "Are You Ready to Share?" *AARP News Bulletin* (November 1989), p. 16.
4. Subak-Sharpe and MacLean, "Prime of Life," p. 60.
5. "Nursing Homes Need Kindly Hands," *Modern Maturity* (December 1989–January 1990), p. 100.
6. "Nursing Homes Need Kindly Hands," p. 100.
7. Don McLeod, "Abuse Abounds," *AARP News Bulletin* (May 1990), p. 10.
8. McLeod, "Abuse Abounds," p. 10.
9. Barbara Coleman, "New Guide Focuses on Nursing Home Quality," *AARP News Bulletin* (November 1988), p. 6.

Chapter 9
1. Richard L. Douglass, *Domestic Mistreatment of the Elderly— Towards Prevention* (AARP, 1987), p. 22.

Chapter 10
1. Cheryl Simon, "A Care Package," *Psychology Today* (April 1988), p. 45.

2. Barbara Coleman, "The Gentle Warriors," *AARP News Bulletin* (July/August 1988), p. 16.

Chapter 11
1. Barbara Deane, *Caring for Your Aging Parents: When Love Is Not Enough* (Colorado Springs: NavPress, 1989), pp. 81–82.

Chapter 12
1. Maggie Kuhn, *Maggie Kuhn on Aging: A Dialogue by Dieter Hessel* (Philadelphia: Westminster Press, 1977), p. 30.

Chapter 13
1. J. Oswald Sanders, *Your Best Years* (Chicago: Moody Press, 1982), p. 88. Used by permission.
2. Peggy Eastman, "A Carrot a Day...," *AARP News Bulletin* (November 1988), p. 2.
3. "The Latest Word On Cholesterol: Too Much Fat Is Too Much Risk," *AARP News Bulletin* (March 1990), p. 2.
4. "Cholesterol," p. 2.
5. Eastman, "A Carrot a Day...," p. 2.
6. Erik H. Erikson, Joan M. Erikson, and Helen Q. Kivnick, *Vital Involvement in Old Age* (New York: W. W. Norton & Co., Inc., 1986).
7. "Three-Year Project to Focus on Frailty," *Orange County Register* (April 6, 1990), p. A6.
8. Robin Marantz Henig, "A Healthy Dose of Exercise," *AARP News Bulletin.*
9. Erikson, et al, *Vital Involvement in Old Age*, p. 314.
10. As quoted by J. Oswald Sanders, *Your Best Years*, p. 90. Used by permission.
11. Erikson, et al, *Vital Involvement in Old Age*, p. 310.
12. Mark Cutshall, "And a Little Child Shall Lead Them," *Focus On the Family* (March 1989), p. 19.
13. Erikson, et al, *Vital Involvement in Old Age*, p. 319.
14. "For Joe, So Much to Learn," *AARP News Bulletin* (October 1989), p. 6.
15. Nancy Kessler, "All for the Wild," *AARP News Bulletin* (October 1989), p. 20.

16. Judith Allen Shelly and Sharon Fish, *Spiritual Care, The Nurse's Role*, Third Edition (Downers Grove, IL: Inter-Varsity Press, 1988), pp. 32–33. Used by permission.

Chapter 14
1. Paul Tournier, *Learn to Grow Old* (San Francisco: Harper-Collins, 1983), pp. 71–72.
2. Florence Littauer, *Your Personality Tree* (Dallas: Word Books, 1986), pp. 213–215. Reprinted by permission.

Chapter 15
1. *Matthew Henry Commentary*, III (McLean, VA: MacDonald Publishing Co., n.d.), p. 907.

Epilogue
1. R. Scott Sullender, *Grief and Growth* (Mahwah, NJ: Paulist Press, 1985), p. 49.